COGAT®
GRADE 1
NON-VERBAL

3 Practice Tests
Level 7

Savant Test Prep™

www.SavantPrep.com

Please leave a review for this book!

Thank you for purchasing this resource.

Please take a moment to leave a
review on the website where you purchased this.

TABLE OF CONTENTS

INTRODUCTION

COGAT® GENERAL INFORMATION

- COGAT® stands for Cognitive Abilities Test®.
- The test measures students' reasoning skills and problem-solving skills.
- It provides educators with an overall assessment of students' academic strengths and weaknesses.
- The COGAT® is commonly used as a screener for gifted and talented programs.
    - Gifted and Talented (G&T) selection sometimes requires a teacher recommendation as well.
- The test is usually administered in a group setting.
- A teacher (or other school associate) administers the test, reading the directions.
- Please check with your school/testing site regarding its testing procedures, as these may differ.

COGAT® LEVEL 7 FORMAT

- Students in first grade take the COGAT® Level 7.
- The Non-Verbal Battery has 44 questions.
- The test is divided into 3 main parts, each called a "Battery." Each Battery has three question types. See the chart below.

VERBAL BATTERY	NON-VERBAL BATTERY	QUANTITATIVE BATTERY
Picture Analogies: 16 Questions	Figure Analogies: 16 Questions	Number Puzzles: 12 Questions
Picture Classification: 16 Questions	Figure Classification: 16 Questions	Number Series: 16 Questions
Sentence Completion: 16 Questions	Paper Folding: 12 Questions	Number Analogies: 16 Questions

- Often, schools administer one Battery per day, allowing approximately 45 minutes per Battery.
- Students have around 15 minutes to complete each question type (for example, students would have around 15 minutes to complete Figure Analogies).
- See the following pages for examples and explanations of each question type.

COGAT® SCORING

- Students receive points for correct answers. Points are not deducted for incorrect answers. (Therefore, students should at least guess versus leaving a question blank.)
- In general, schools have a "cut-off" COGAT® score, which they consider together with additional criteria, for gifted & talented acceptance. This varies by school.
- This score is usually at least 98%. (However, some schools accept scores of 95% or even 85%.)
- A score of 98% means that your child scored as well as, or better than, 98% of those in his/her testing group.
- COGAT® scores are available for the entire test and can be broken down by Battery.
- Depending on the school/program, such a "cut-off" score may only be required on one or two of the Batteries (and not on the test overall).
- It is essential to check with your school/program for their acceptance procedures.
- The COGAT® Practice Tests in this book can not yield these percentiles because they have not been given to a large enough group of students to produce an accurate comparison/calculation.

HOW TO USE THIS BOOK

1. Go over the Question Examples together with your child. These begin on the next page.

2. Do Practice Test 1 (Workbook Format)
   - Do these questions with your child, especially if this is your child's first exposure to COGAT®-prep questions. These questions have a "workbook format," meaning they are meant to be done together.
   - Do <u>not</u> assign a time limit.
   - Talk about what the question is asking your child to do.
   - Questions progress in difficulty. (The first few questions are quite simple.)
   - Go over the answers using the Answer Key.
   - For questions missed, go over the answers again, discussing what makes the correct answer better than the other choices.

3. Do the remaining Practice Tests following Practice Test 1.
   - If your child progressed easily through Practice Test 1, see how well they can do without your help.
   - If your child needed assistance with much of Practice Test 1, then continue to assist your child with Practice Test 2.
   - If you wish to assign a time limit, assign around 15 minutes per question type.
   - Go over the answers using the Answer Key.
   - For questions missed, go over the answers again, discussing what makes the correct answer better than the other choices.

4. **Need more practice?**

   - **Help your child ace the test!**

   - **Check out Savant Test Prep™ books on Amazon®.**

TEST-TAKING TIPS

- Ensure your child listens carefully to the directions.
- Make sure (s)he does not rush through questions. (There is no prize for finishing first!) Tell your child to look carefully at the question. Then, tell your child to look at each answer choice before marking his/her answer.
  - If you notice your child continuing to rush through the questions, tell him/her to point to each part of the question. Then, point to each answer choice.
- If (s)he does not know the answer, then use the process of elimination. Cross out any answer choices which are clearly incorrect, then choose from those remaining.
- This tip/suggestion is entirely at <u>your</u> discretion. You may wish to offer some sort of special motivation to encourage your child to do his/her best. An extra incentive of, for example, an art set, a building block set, or a special outing can go a long way in motivating young learners!
- The night before testing, make sure your child has enough sleep, without any interruptions. (Think about the difference in **your** brain function with a good night's sleep vs. without. The same goes for your child's.)
- The morning before the test, ensure your child eats a healthy breakfast with protein and complex carbs. Do not let them eat sugar, chocolate, etc.
- If you can choose the time your child will take the test (for example, if (s)he will take the test individually, instead of at school with a group), opt for a morning testing session, when your child will be most alert.

QUESTION EXAMPLES

- Here is an overview of the COGAT® question types.
- This section has <u>simple</u> examples, to introduce your child to test concepts.
    - Do these examples together with your child.
- Below the questions are explanations for parents.

1. FIGURE ANALOGIES (NON-VERBAL BATTERY)

• **Directions (read to child):** The pictures in the top boxes go together in some way. Look at the bottom boxes. One box is empty. Look at the row of pictures next to the boxes. These are the answer choices. Which one of these choices goes with the picture in the bottom box like the pictures in the top box go together?

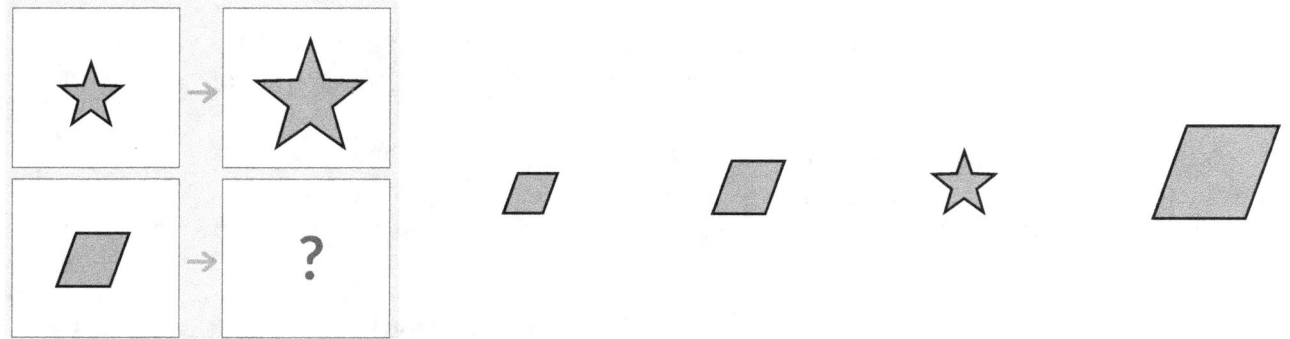

• **Using this question as an example, say to your child:** In the top left box, we see 1 star. In the top right box, we also see a star, but it has gotten bigger. Let's come up with a rule to describe how the picture has changed from left to right. From left to right, the shape gets bigger. On the bottom is a parallelogram. Let's look at the answer choices and see if any fit our rule. The first choice does not - the shape is smaller. The second choice does not - the shape is the same size. The third choice does not - it is a different shape. The last choice does - it is the same shape as the bottom box, but it is bigger.

• **Explanation (for parents):** In the directions, the word "picture" means a "figure" consisting of one or more shapes/lines/etc.

Your child must figure out how the images in top set of boxes are related and belong together. Then, (s)he must figure out which answer choice would go with the bottom left image so that the bottom set would have the same analogous relationship as the top set. (The small arrows demonstrate that the images go together.)

Try to define a "rule" to describe how the top set belongs together.

Make your "rule" describe a "change" that occurs from the top left box to the top right box.

Next, take this "rule" describing the change, and apply it to the bottom picture.

Then, look at the answer choices to determine which one would make the bottom set also follow your "rule."

If more than one answer choice fits the rule, then the rule needs to be more specific.

• The images below outline "changes" in Figure Analogy questions (how the figures change in the analogy).

• In basic Figure Analogy questions, like the example, there is one "change" -or- a change that is quite obvious.

• In the below images #1-9, there is one change.

• More advanced questions, like #10-12 below, have two changes (or changes that are not as obvious).

Directions for the below images:
• See if your child can figure out how the first picture "changes" to the second picture below.
• The questions' "change" (the logic) is at the bottom of the page.

1.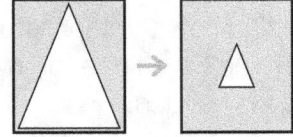

2.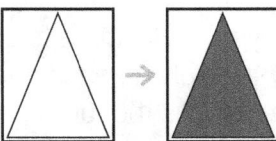

3.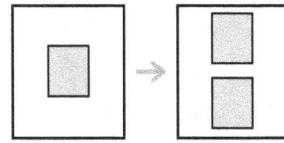

4.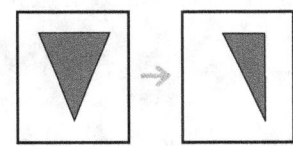

5.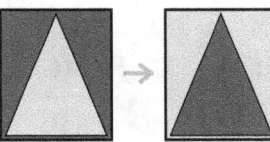

6.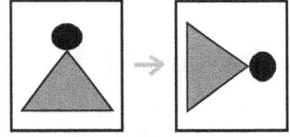

7.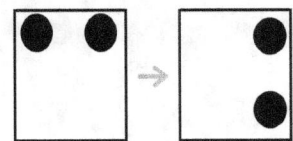

8.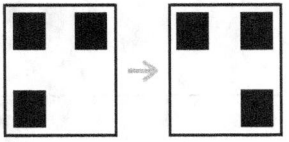

9.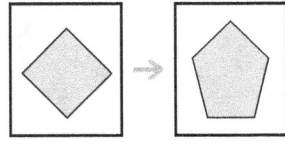

10.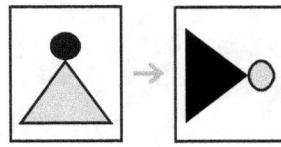

11.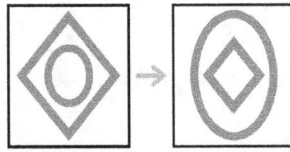

12.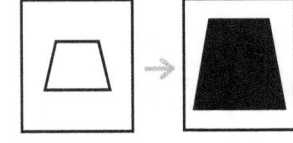

1. Size (gets smaller)
2. Color (white to dark gray)
3. Quantity (plus 1)
4. Whole to Half
5. Color Reversal
6. Rotation (clockwise, 90°)

7. Rotation (clockwise, 90°)
8. Rotation -or- Mirror Image/"Flip"
9. Number of Shape Sides (shape with +1 side)
10. Two Changes: Rotation (clockwise, 90°)
    and Color Reversal
11. Two Changes: Shape Position and Size
12. Two Changes: Shape Size and Color

2. FIGURE CLASSIFICATION (NON-VERBAL BATTERY)

• **Directions (read to child):** The top row shows three pictures that are alike in some way. Look at the bottom row. There are four pictures. Which picture in the bottom row goes best with the pictures in the top row?

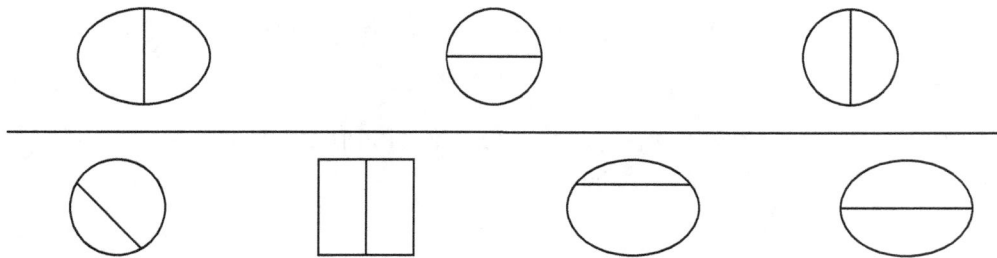

• **Explanation (for parents):** Together with your child, try to figure out a "rule" describing how the top pictures are alike and belong together. Then, apply the "rule" to each answer choice to determine which one follows it. If your child finds that more than one choice follows the rule, then a more specific rule is needed.

• **Using the above question as an example, say to your child:** Here we see 1 oval divided in half, 1 circle divided in half, and 1 circle divided in half. What is a rule that describes how they are alike? They are all round and divided in half. In the bottom row, which choice follows this rule? Choice 1 and 3 are round and divided, but not divided in half. Choice 2 is divided in half, but it is not round. Choice 4 is round and divided in half.

• The following examples include basic logic used in Figure Classification questions, with answers at the end.

• **Directions (read to child):** The top row shows three pictures that are alike in some way. Look at the bottom row. There are four pictures. Which picture in the bottom row goes best with the pictures in the top row?

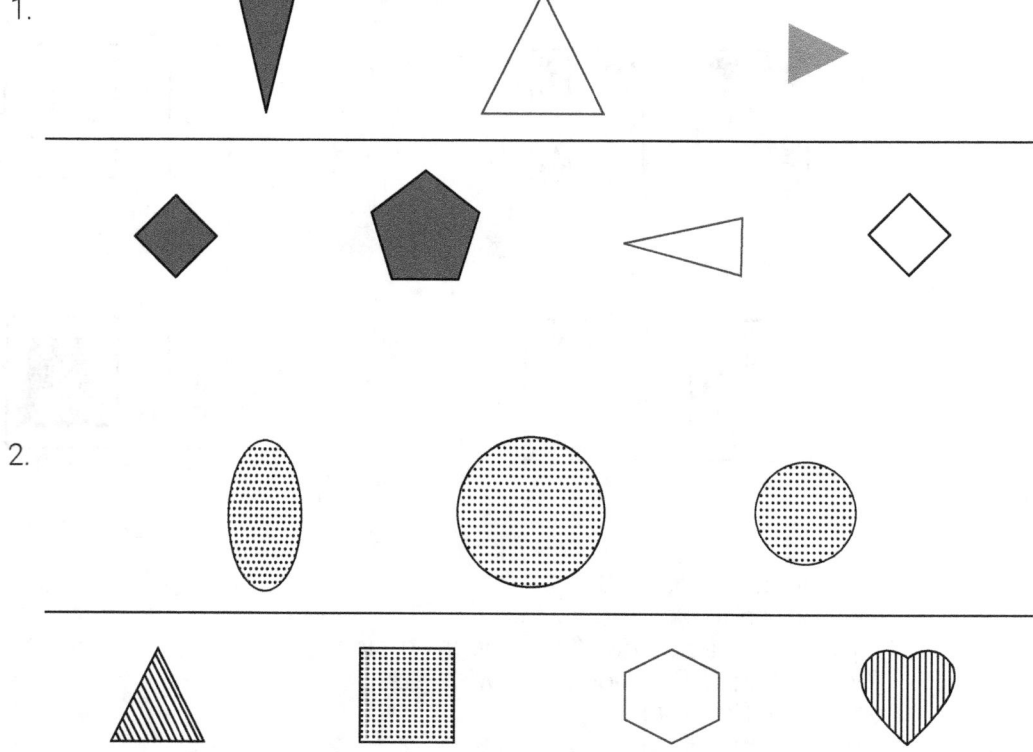

1.

2.

• **Note:** These are <u>more challenging</u>. If your child needs help, ask them the question next to the number.

3. Which way is it pointing?

4. What is the design inside?

5. How much is black? How much is white?

6. How many sides?

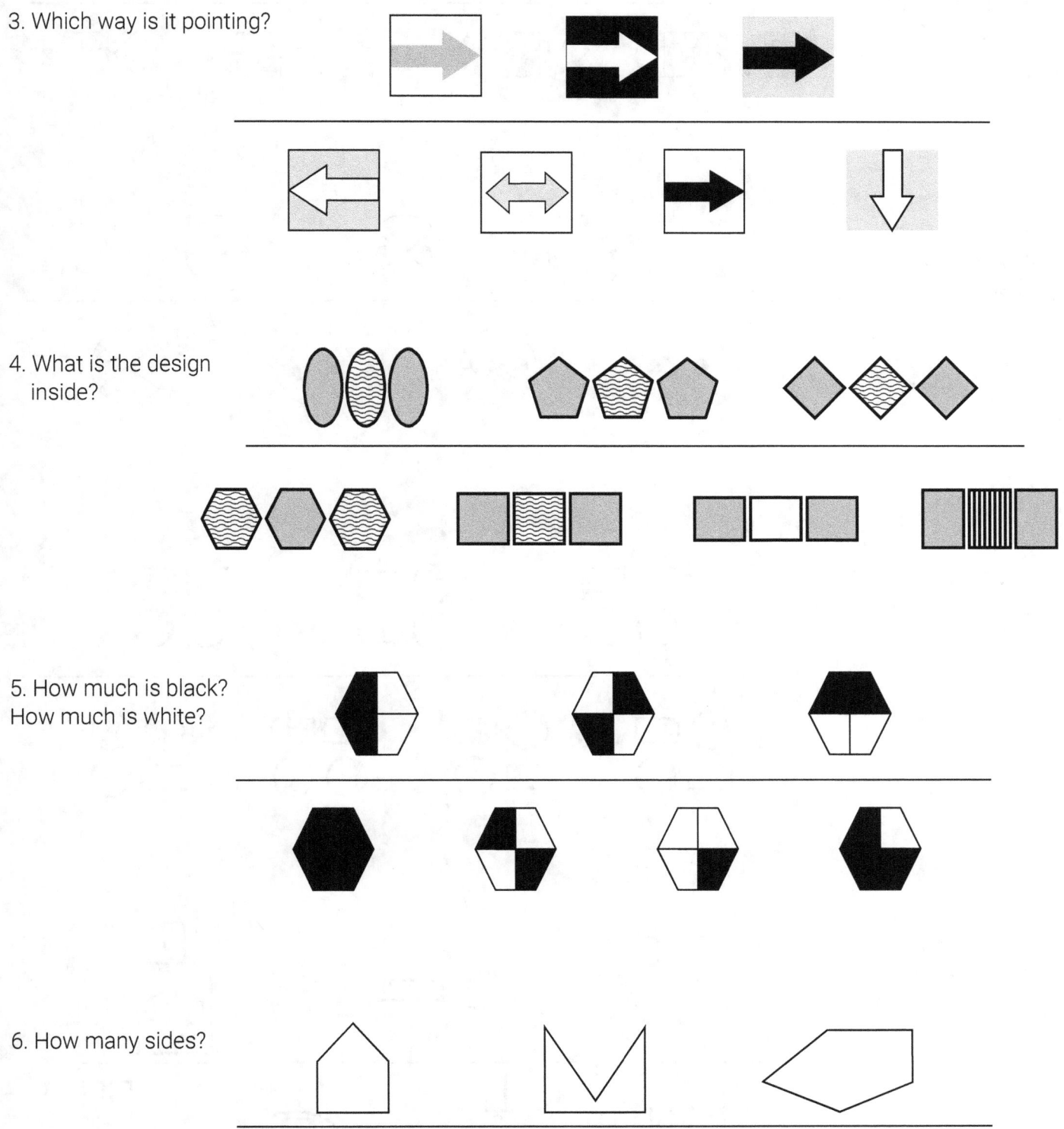

1- Choice 3: triangles
2- Choice 2: filled with dots
3- Choice 3: arrows point right
4- Choice 2: the designs are gray, wavy lines, gray
5- Choice 2: half is white, half is black
6- Choice 4: the shapes have 5 sides

7. How many shapes of each kind are together next to each other?

   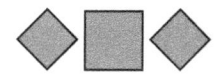

8. What kind of small shapes are there?

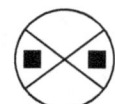  

9. What kinds of shape are gray or white? How many?

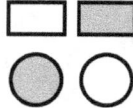 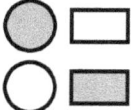 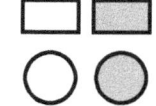

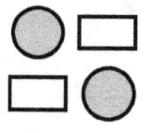 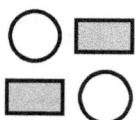 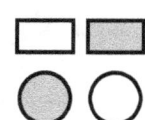 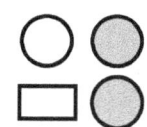

10. How many shapes are in each group?

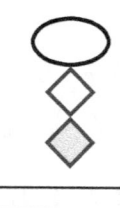 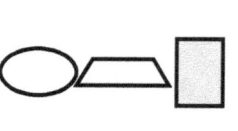 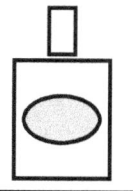

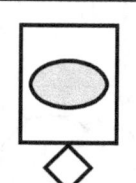 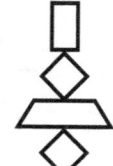 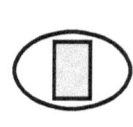 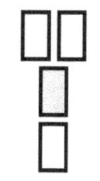

7- Choice 3: there are 2 identical shapes next to a shape that's a different kind of shape
8- Choice 4: the 2 small black shapes are the same
9- Choice 3: the 2 gray shapes are 1 rectangle and 1 circle   10- Choice 1: there are 3 shapes in the group

10

3. PAPER FOLDING (NON-VERBAL BATTERY)

• **Directions (read to child):** The top row of pictures shows a sheet of paper. The paper was folded, then something was cut out. Which picture in the bottom row shows how the paper would look after it's unfolded?

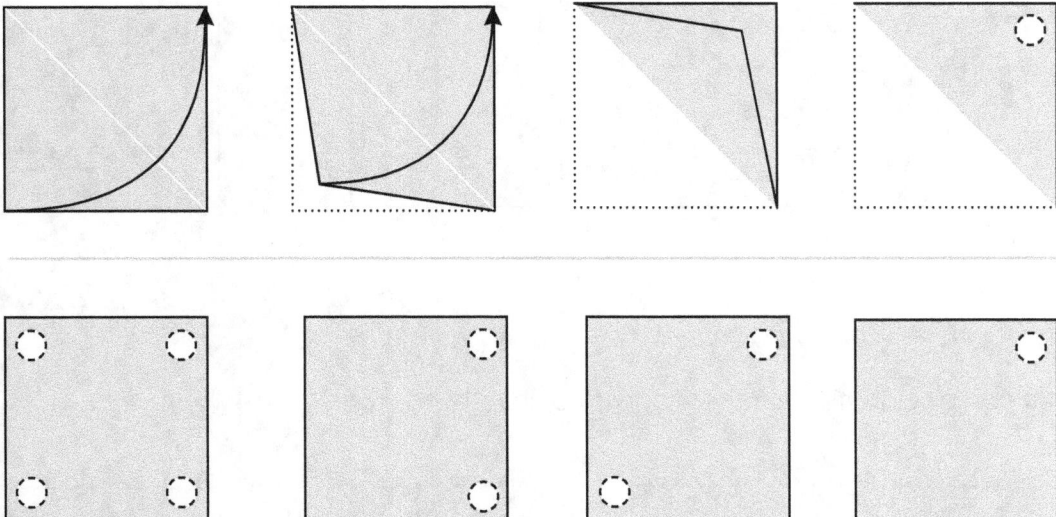

• **Explanation (read to child):** The first choice has too many holes. In the second choice, the holes are not in the correct position. The third choice has the correct number of holes and in the correct position. The last choice only shows the hole on top.

• **Tip:** If Paper Folding is challenging for your child, demonstrate using real paper and scissors. (It is common for kids to initially struggle with Paper Folding. It is not an activity most children have much experience with.)

• Show your child the following examples. Demonstrate using real paper, if needed.

Paper Folding Steps   Result

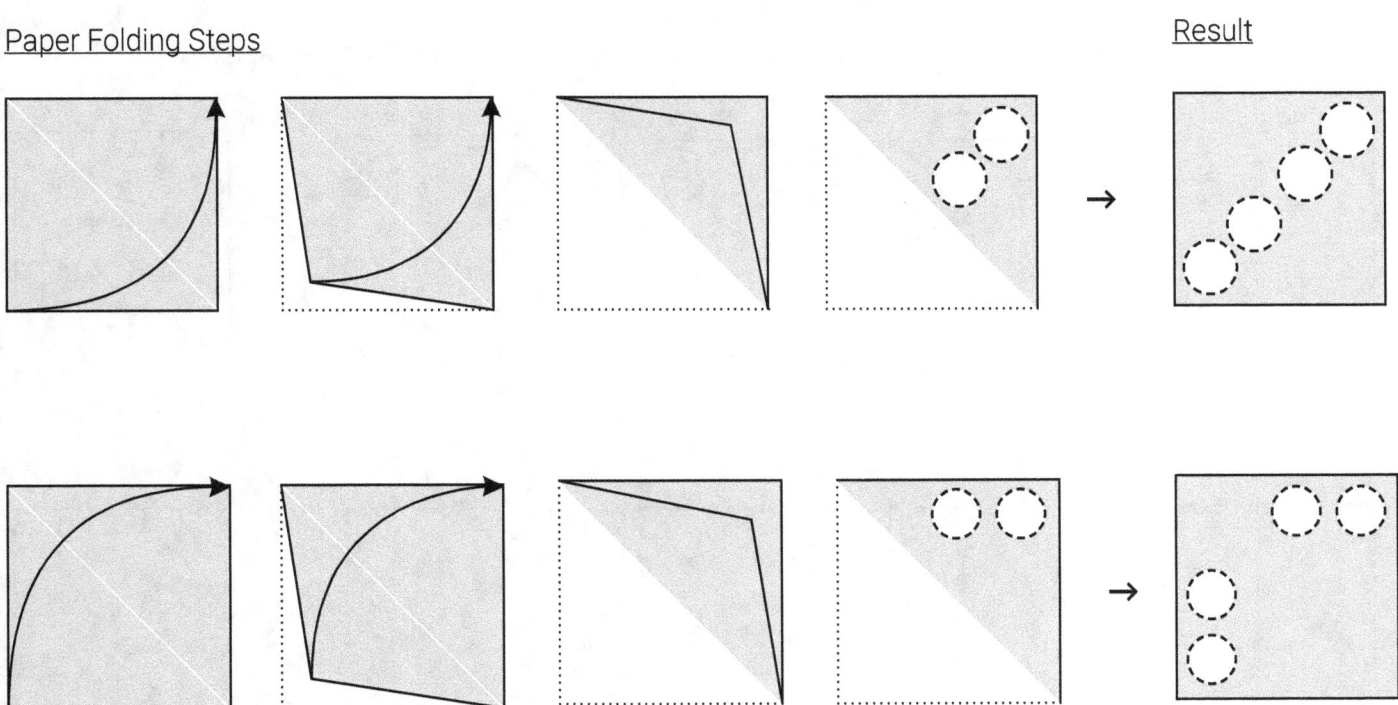

(In the question at the top of the page, the third choice is correct.)

In the example below, point out to your child that when the paper is unfolded the triangles point toward each other.

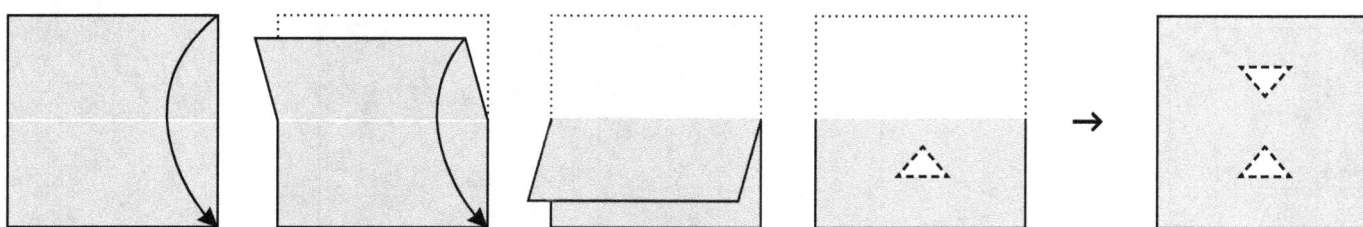

In the example below, point out to your child that the shape is cut into the fold line.

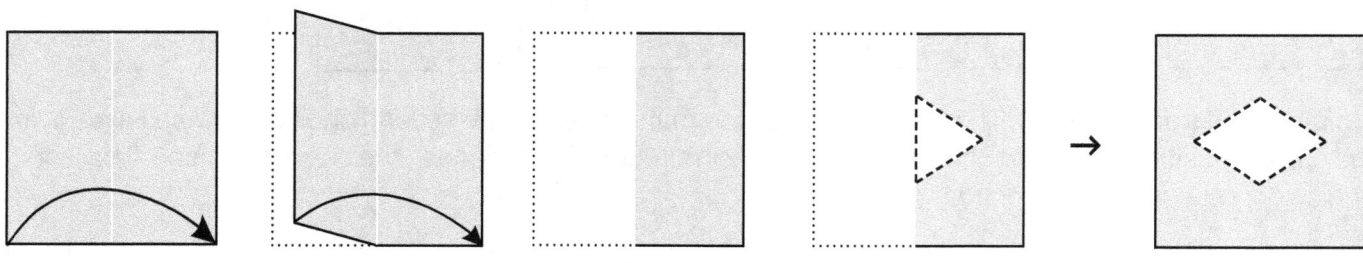

In the examples below, point out to your child how the paper is folded, and then folded again.

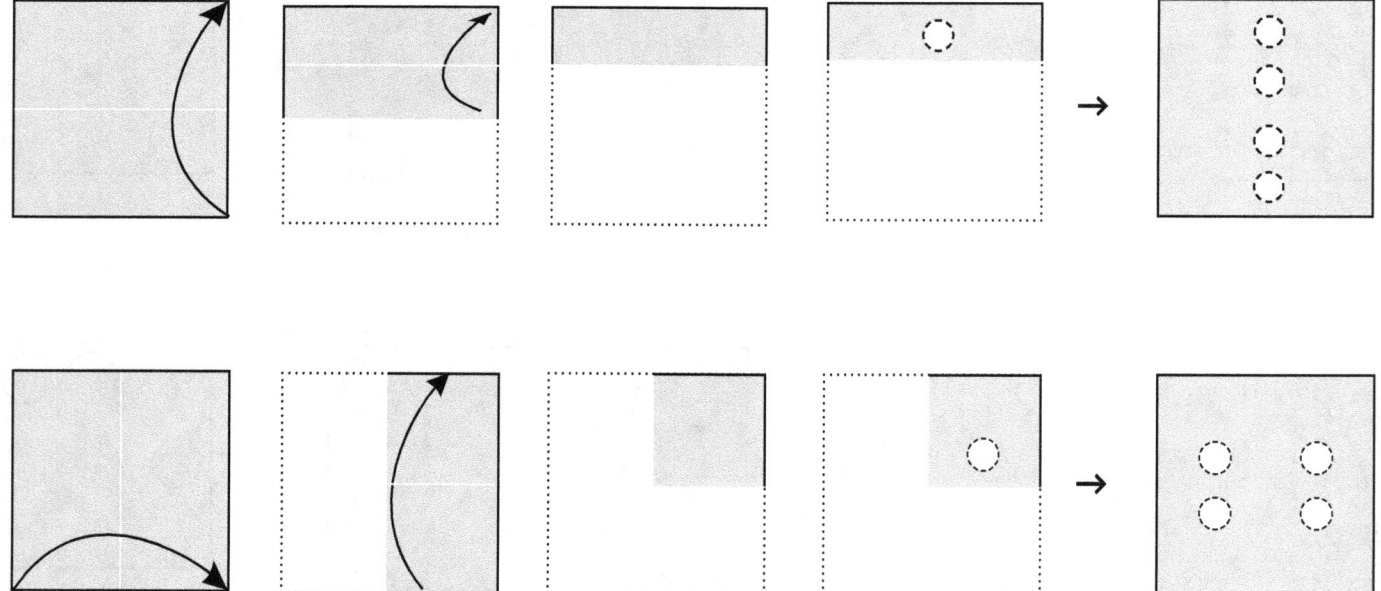

Parents, read the below with your child.

Watch out!

This book is filled with tricky questions. Can you answer them?

Of course you can!

Pay close attention to each question and try your best.

We'll be here to help you along the way!

Practice Test 1 (Workbook Format) begins on the next page.

FIGURE ANALOGIES

What goes in the empty box?

Sara

Directions (read to child): The pictures in the top boxes go together in some way. Look at the bottom boxes. One box is empty. Look at the row of pictures next to the boxes. These are the answer choices. Which one of these choices goes with the picture in the bottom box like the pictures in the top boxes go together?

Explanation (for parents): A more detailed explanation and a Figure Analogies example question is on p. 6. If you have not already, look over p. 6. Try to define a "rule" to describe how the top set belongs together. With Figure Analogies, this "rule" could describe a "change" that occurs from the top left box to the top right box. Next, take this "rule" describing the change, and apply it to the bottom picture.

Example (read this to child): In the first box, we see a white square. In the second box, we see a square, but this time the top is white and the bottom is gray. Our rule is that the same white shape from the first box is in the second box, but in the second box the top is white and the bottom is gray.

Let's look in the bottom box. We see another white shape. Which answer choice follows our rule? Find the choice that shows the same shape as the first box, but it has a white top and a gray bottom. Choice C is the right answer.

1.

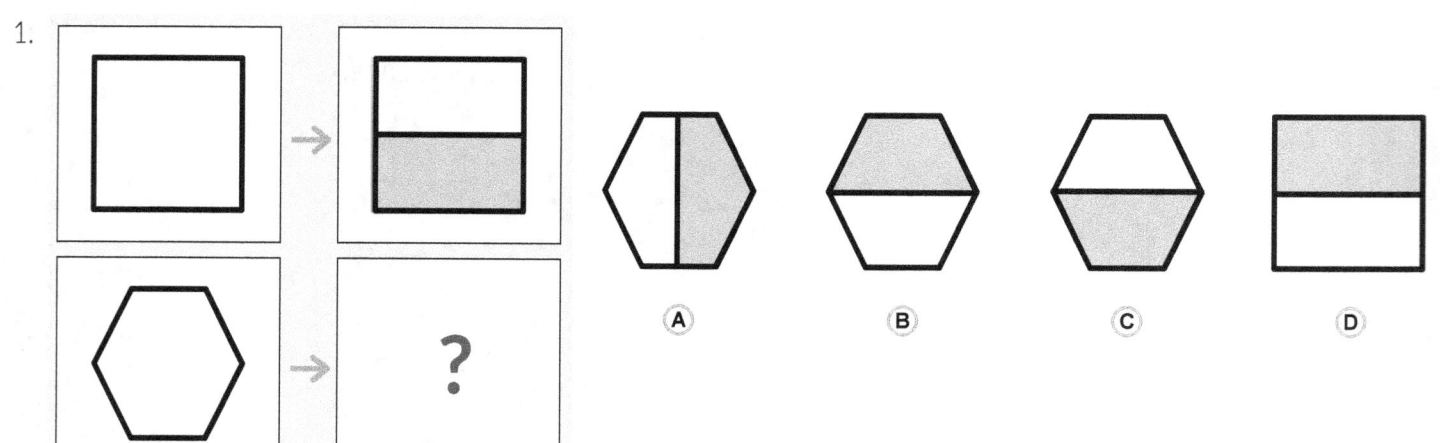

2.

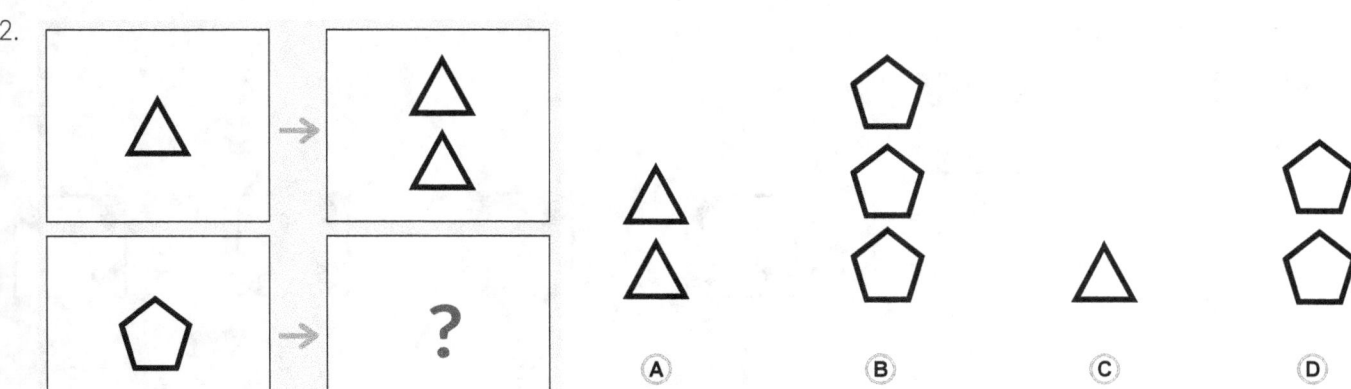

3.

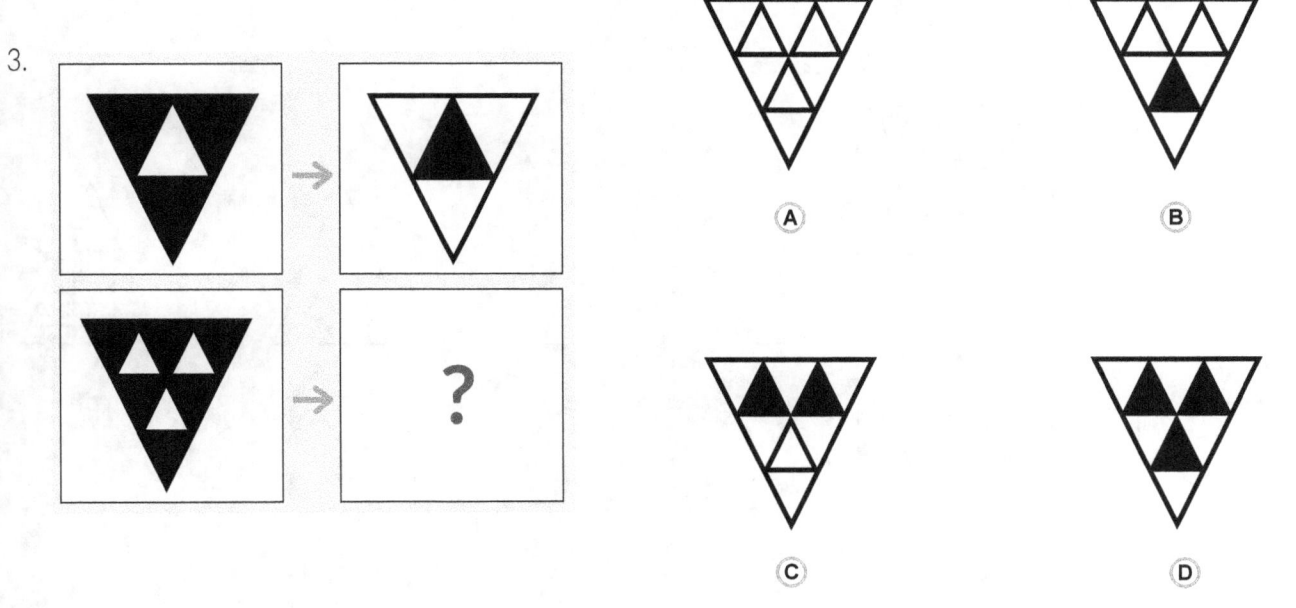

4.

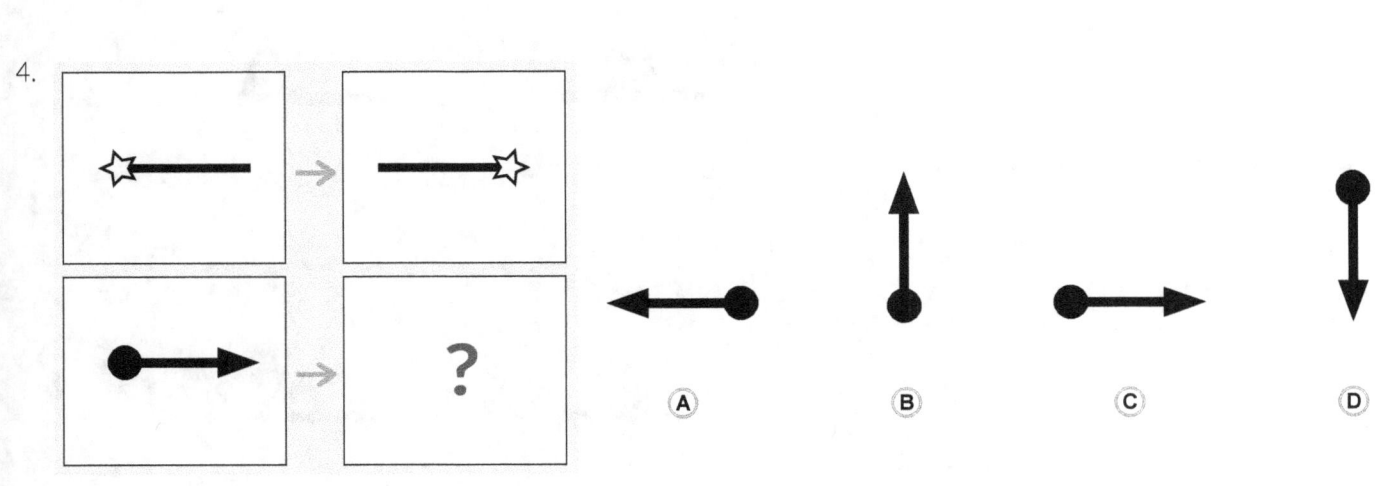

5.

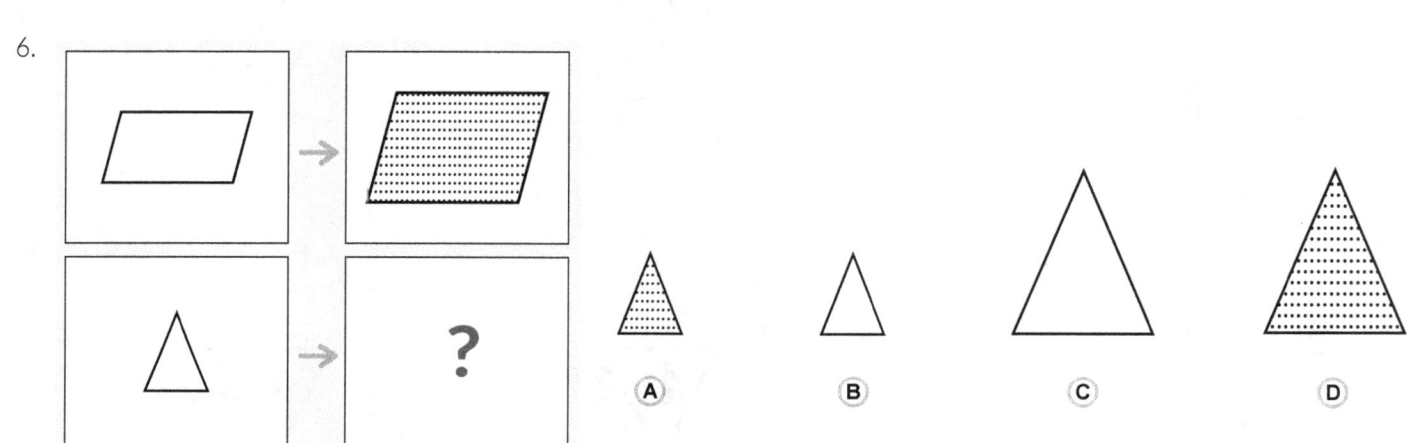

6.

7.

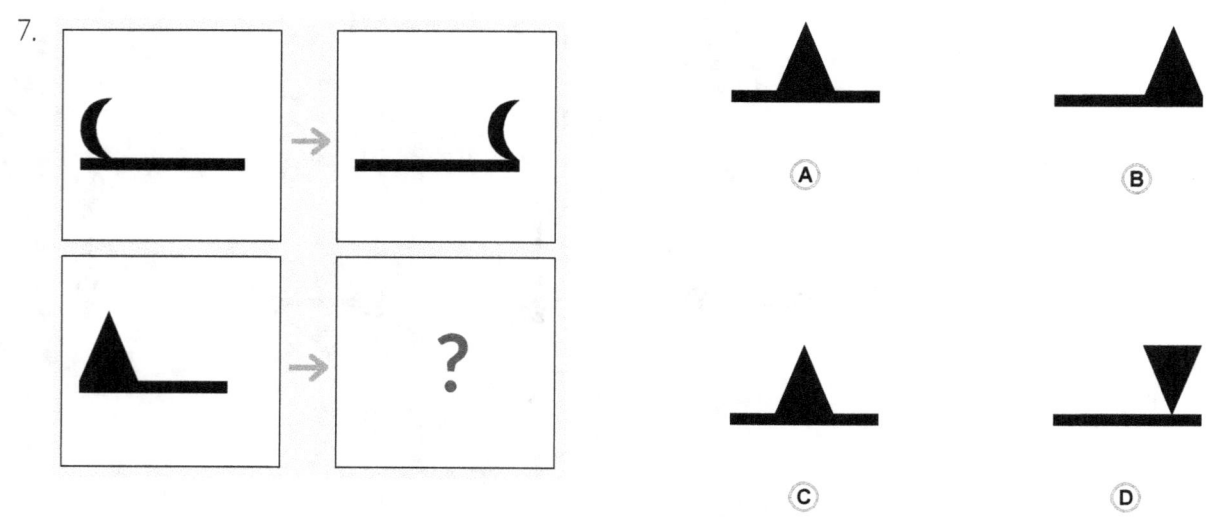

8.

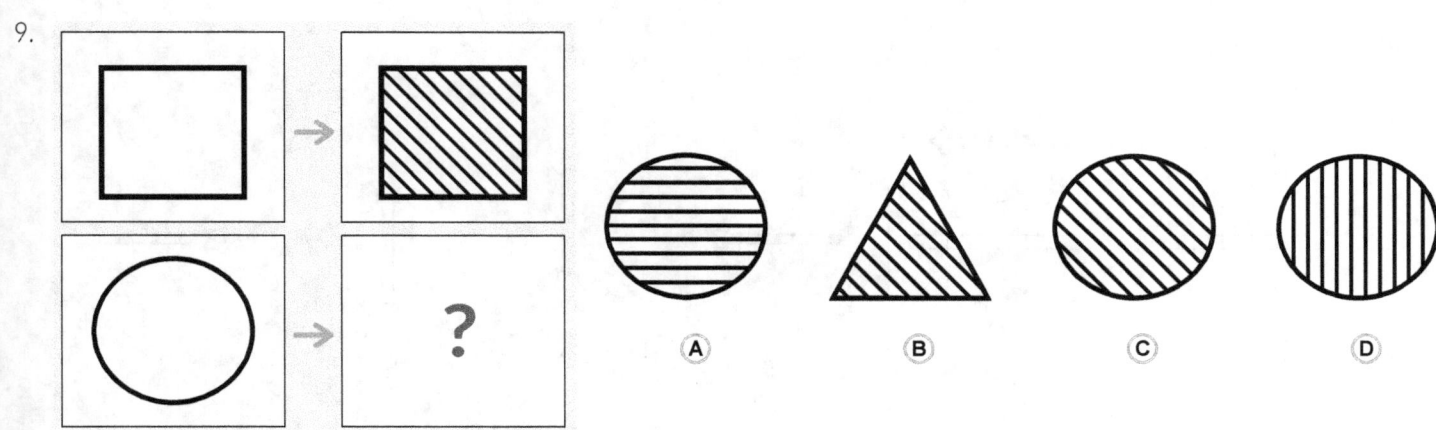

9.

10.

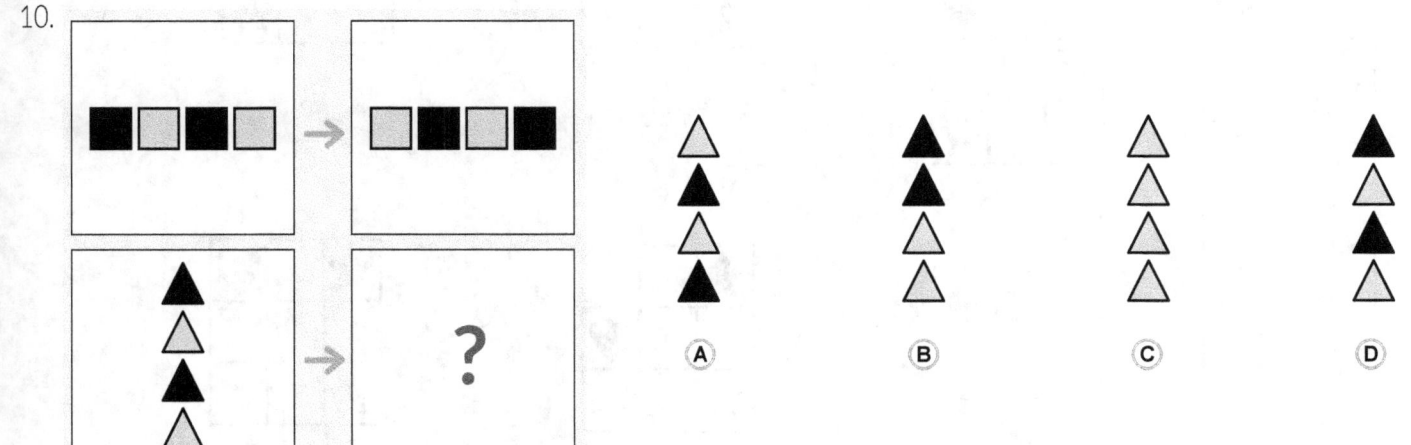

11.

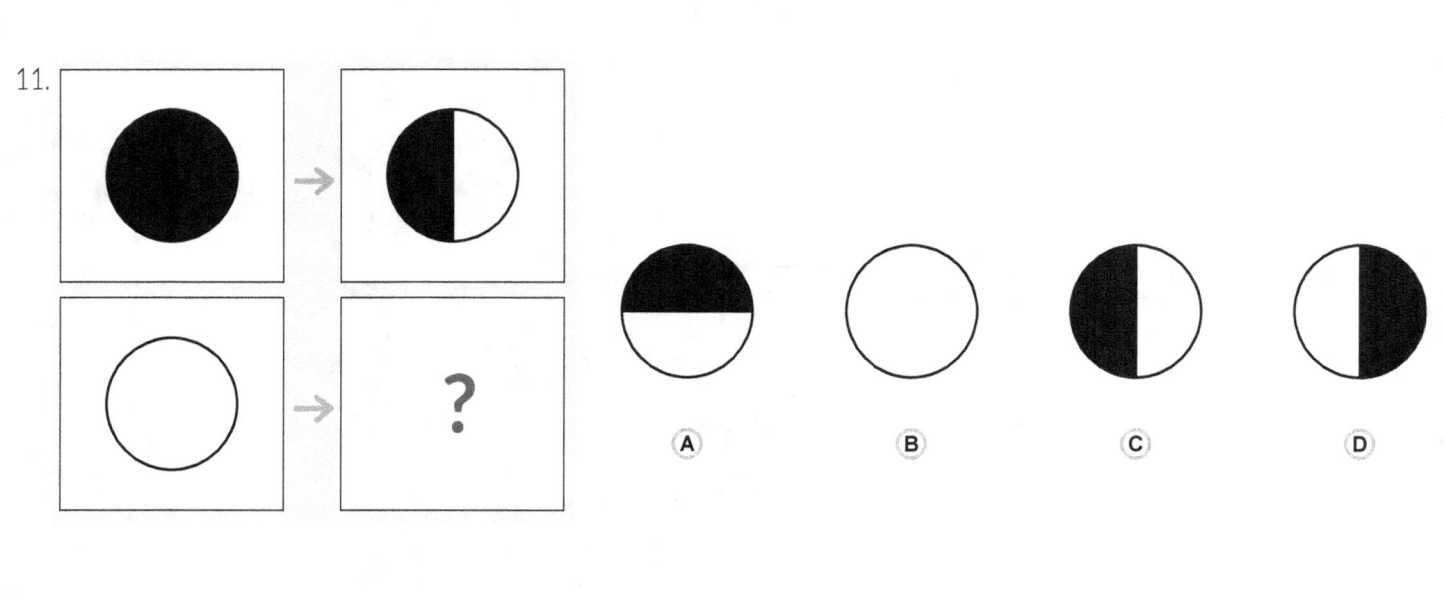

12.

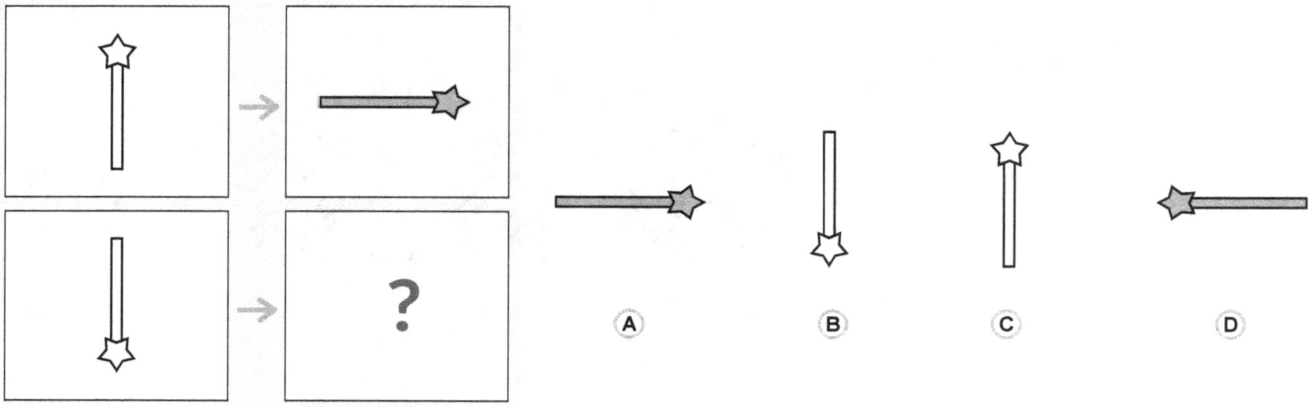

13.

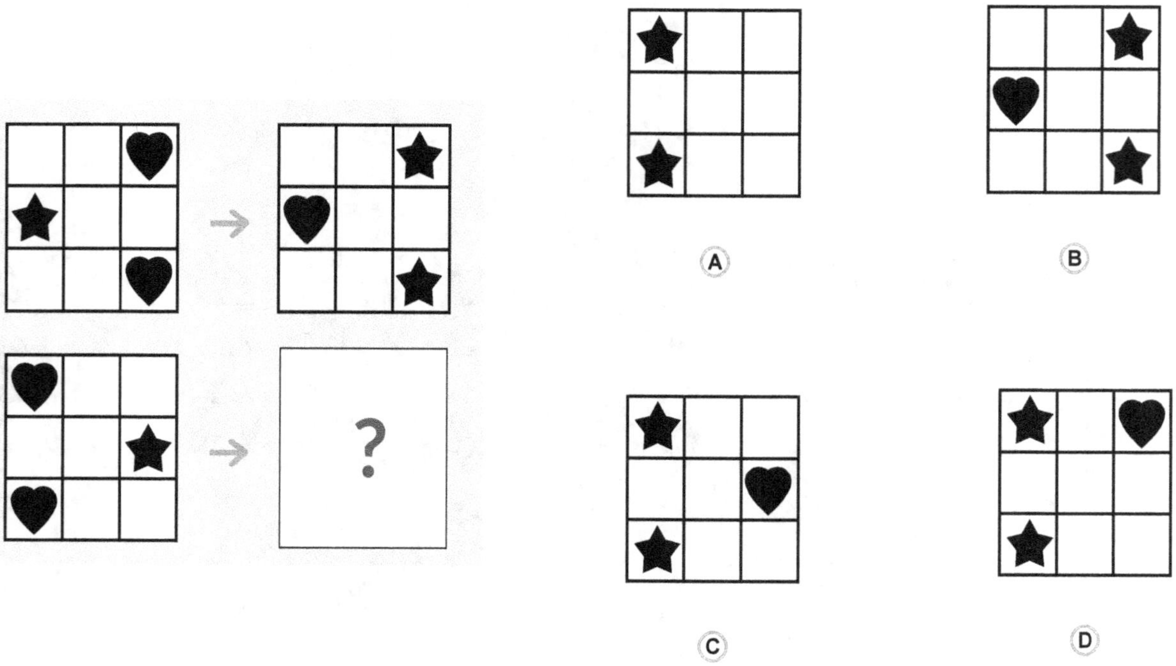

14.

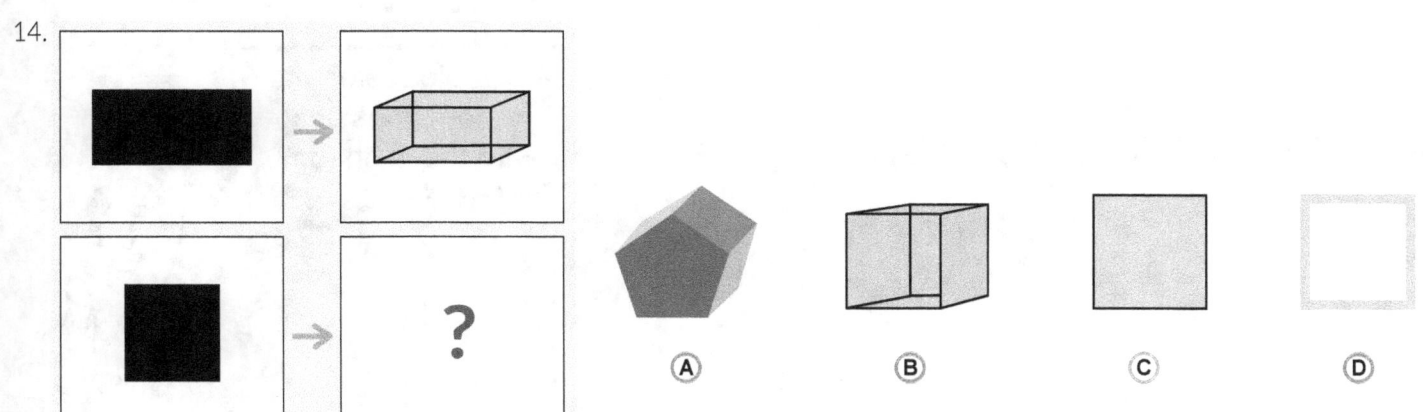

15.

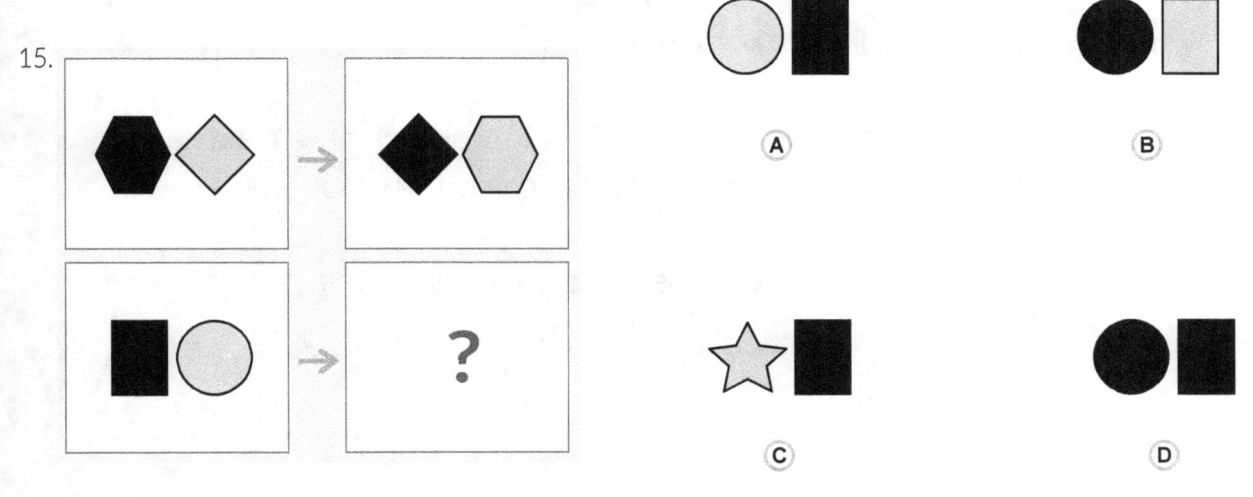

16.

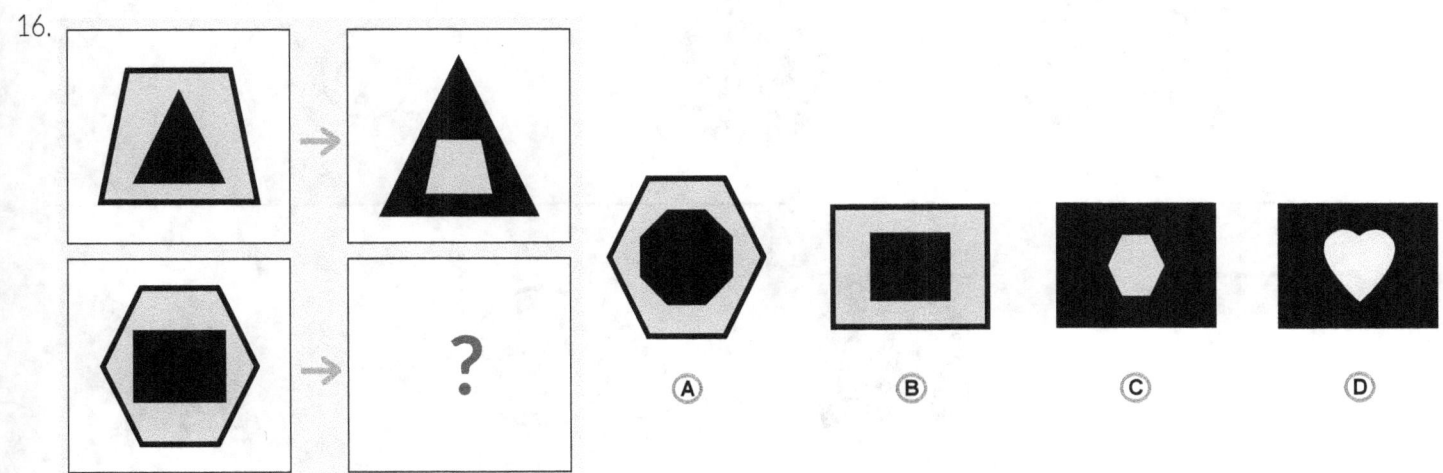

19

FIGURE CLASSIFICATION

What picture on the bottom goes best with those on top?

Kai

Directions (read to child): The top row shows three pictures that are alike in some way. Look at the bottom row. There are four pictures. Which picture in the bottom row goes best with the pictures in the top row?

Explanation (for parents): A more detailed explanation of Figure Classification questions is on p.8. If you have not already, look over p.8. Following is an excerpt.

Together with your child, try to figure out a "rule" describing how the top pictures are alike and belong together. Then, apply the "rule" to each answer choice to determine which one follows it.

If your child finds that more than one choice follows the rule, then a more specific rule is needed. The "rule" for number 1 would be "is a circle." Choice C is the answer.

1.

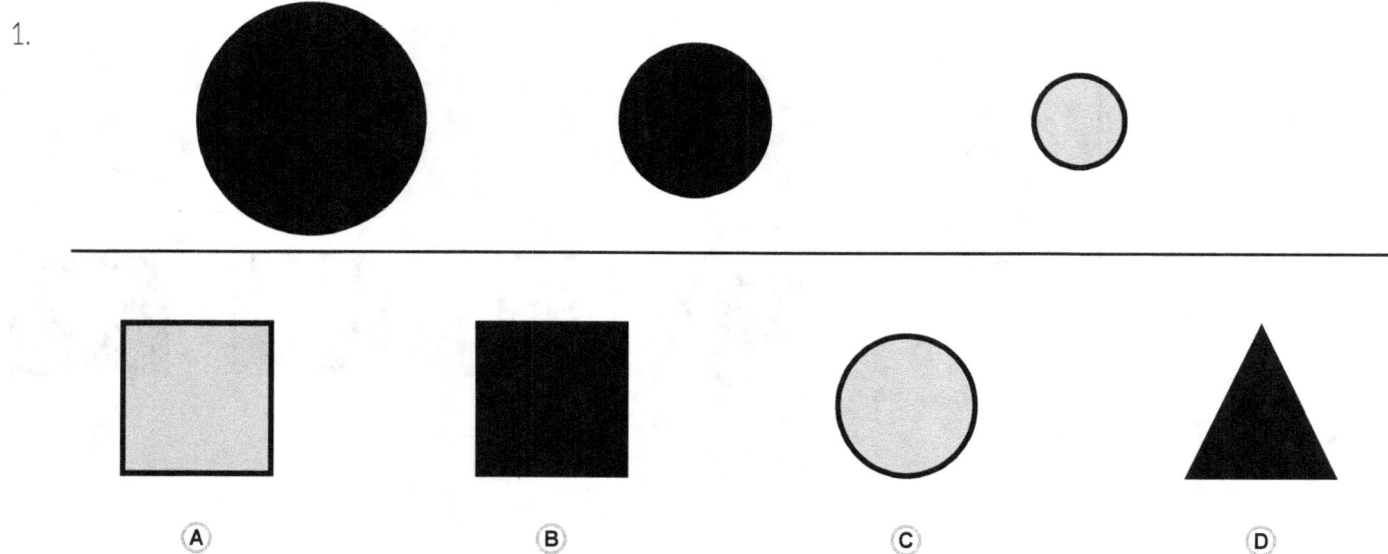

2.

 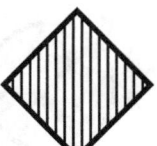 

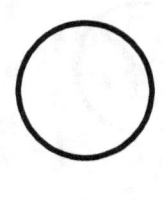

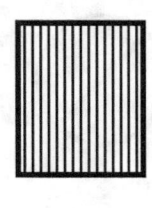

Ⓐ Ⓑ Ⓒ Ⓓ

3.

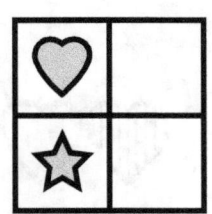  

Ⓐ Ⓑ Ⓒ Ⓓ

4.

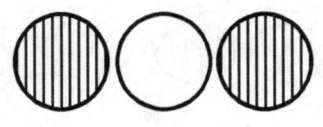 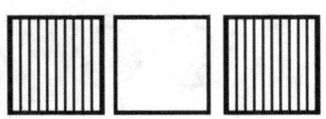 

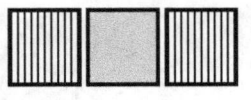 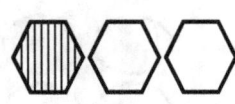 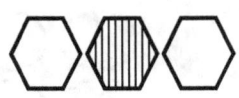 

Ⓐ Ⓑ Ⓒ Ⓓ

5.

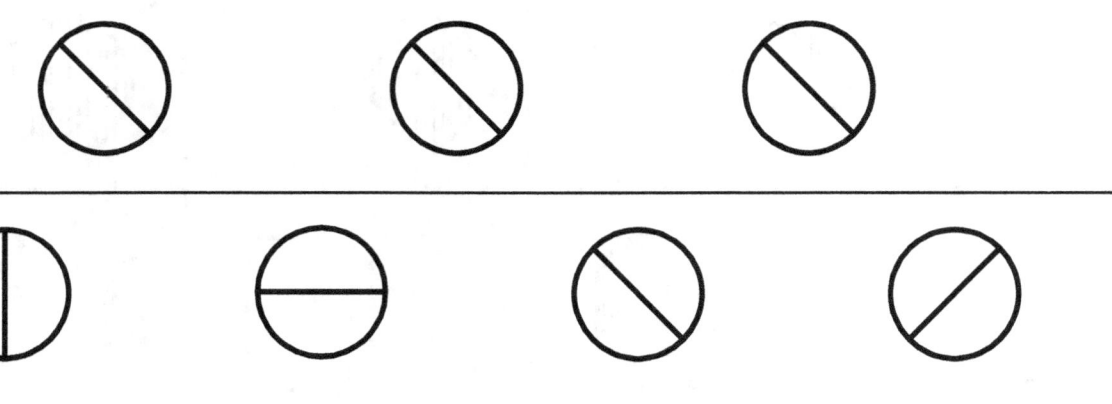

| A | B | C | D |

6.

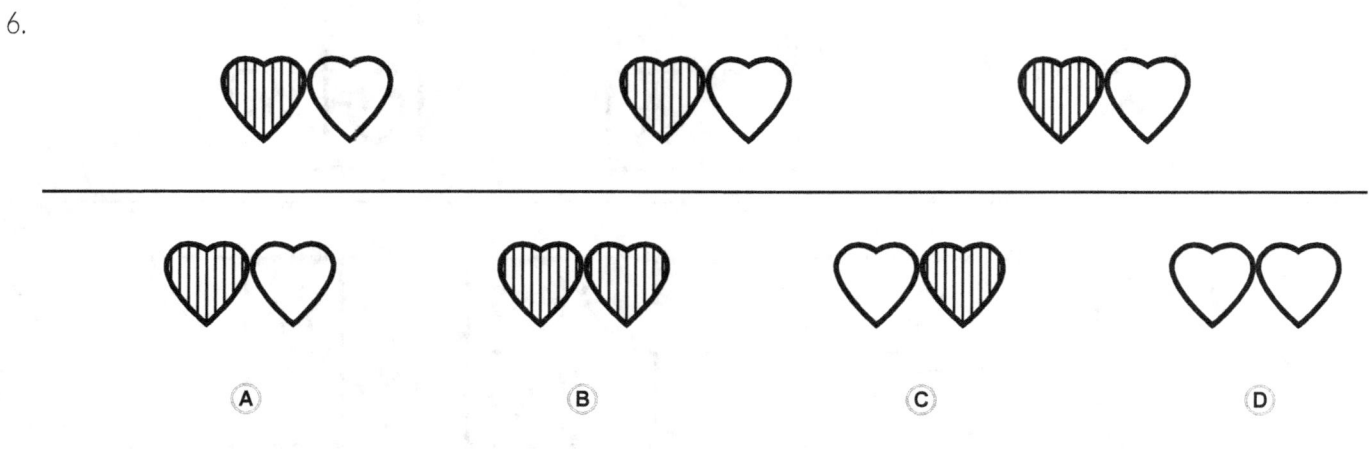

| A | B | C | D |

7.

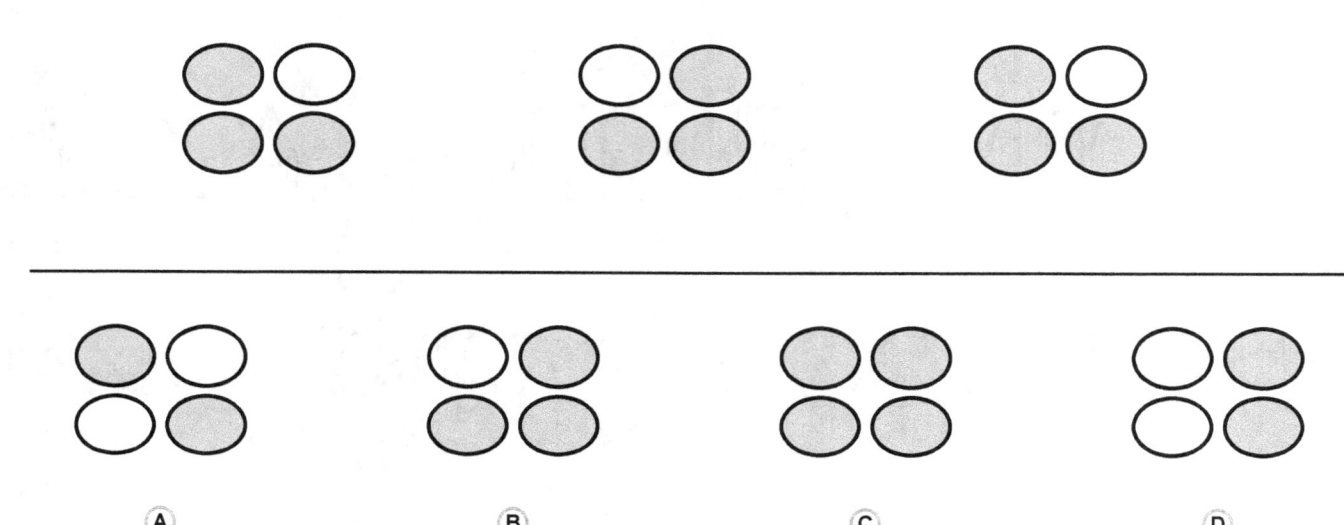

| A | B | C | D |

22

8.

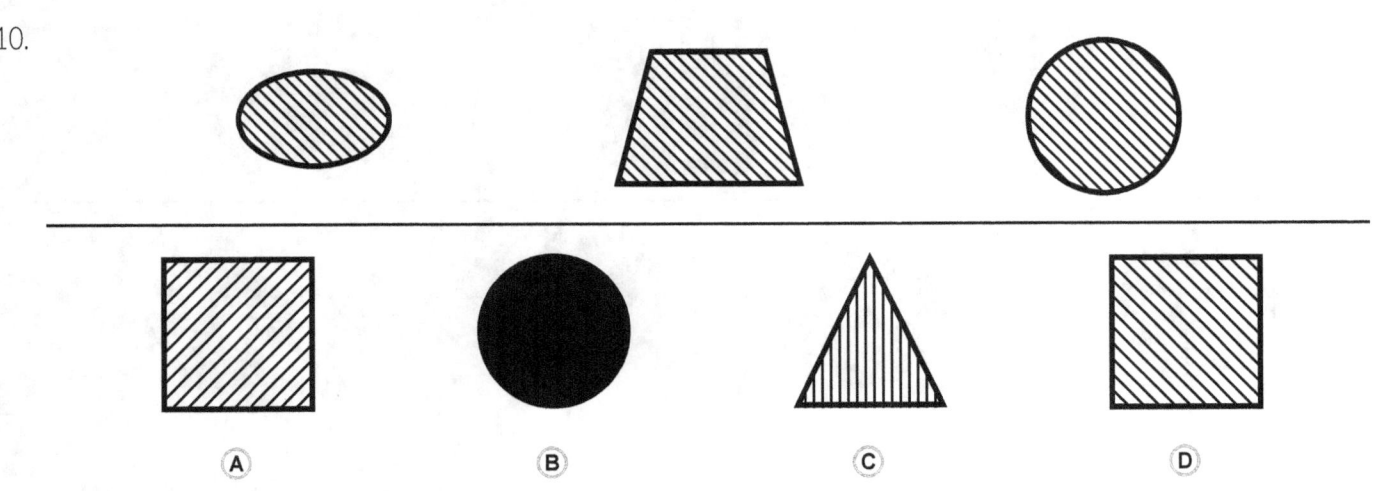

A   B   C   D

9.

A   B   C   D

10.

A   B   C   D

11.

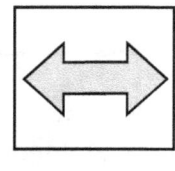 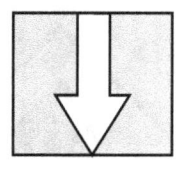

(A)   (B)   (C)   (D)

12.

 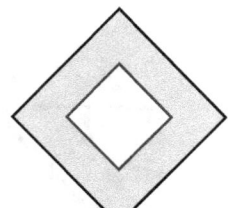 

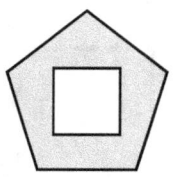 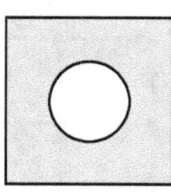 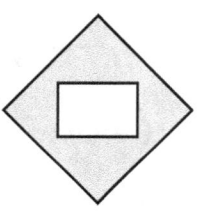 

(A)   (B)   (C)   (D)

13.

  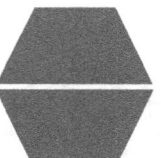

 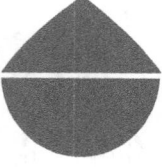  

(A)   (B)   (C)   (D)

14.

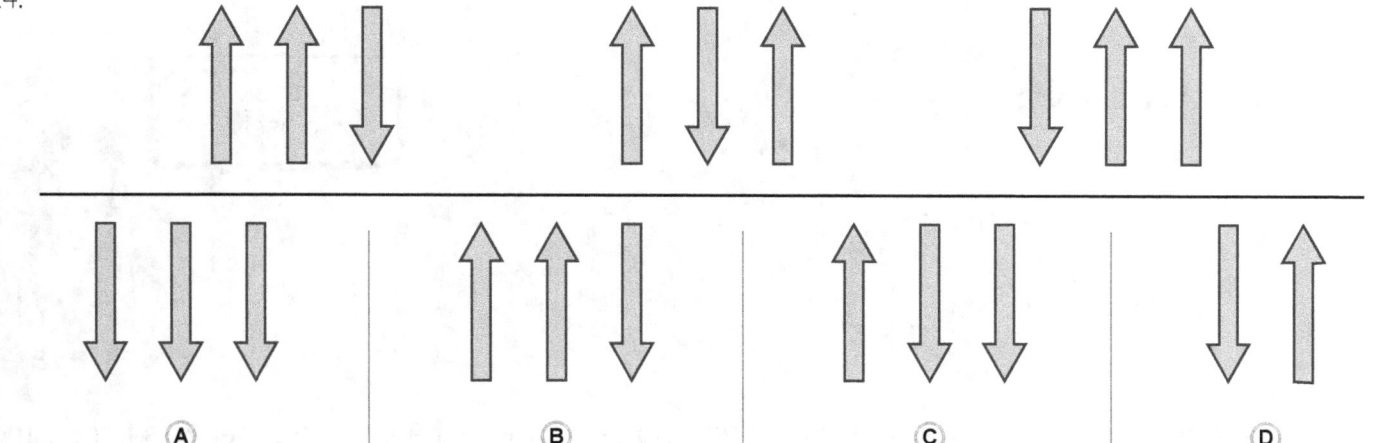

15.

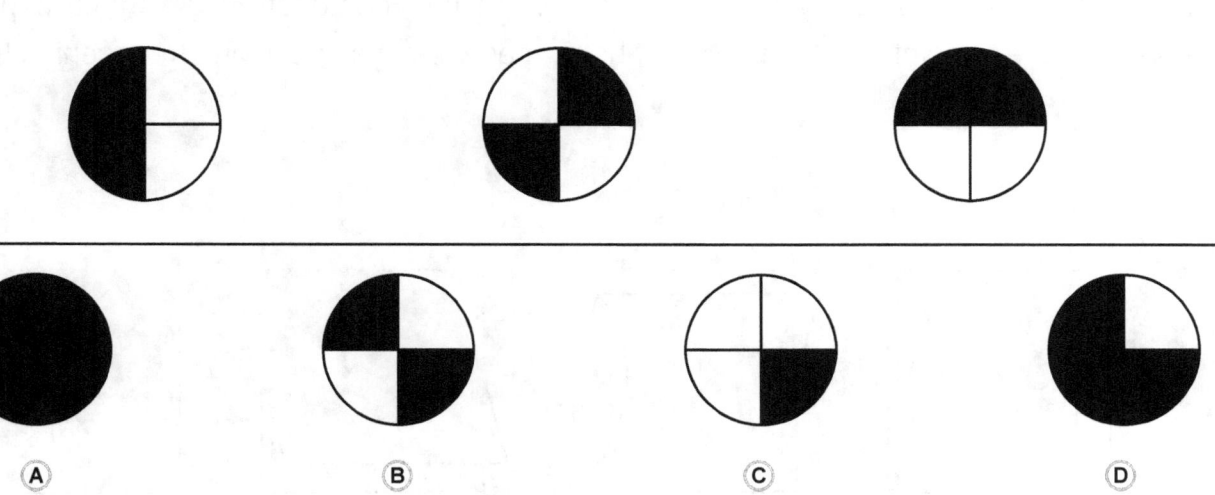

16.

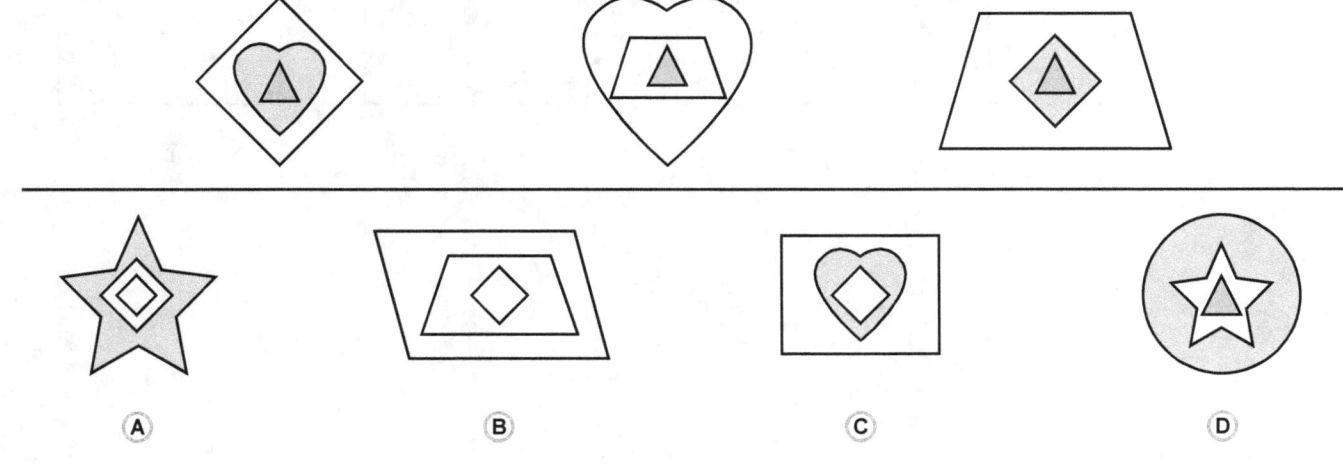

PAPER FOLDING

Look closely!

Maya

Directions (read to child): The top row of pictures shows a sheet of paper. The paper was folded, then something was cut out. Which picture in the bottom row shows how the paper would look after it's unfolded?

Additional information (for parents): As explained earlier on p. 11, children may be initially be "stumped" by Paper Folding. If your child needs help, then try demonstrating with real paper and a hole puncher. Be sure to point out the number of holes made and their position after opening the paper.

1.

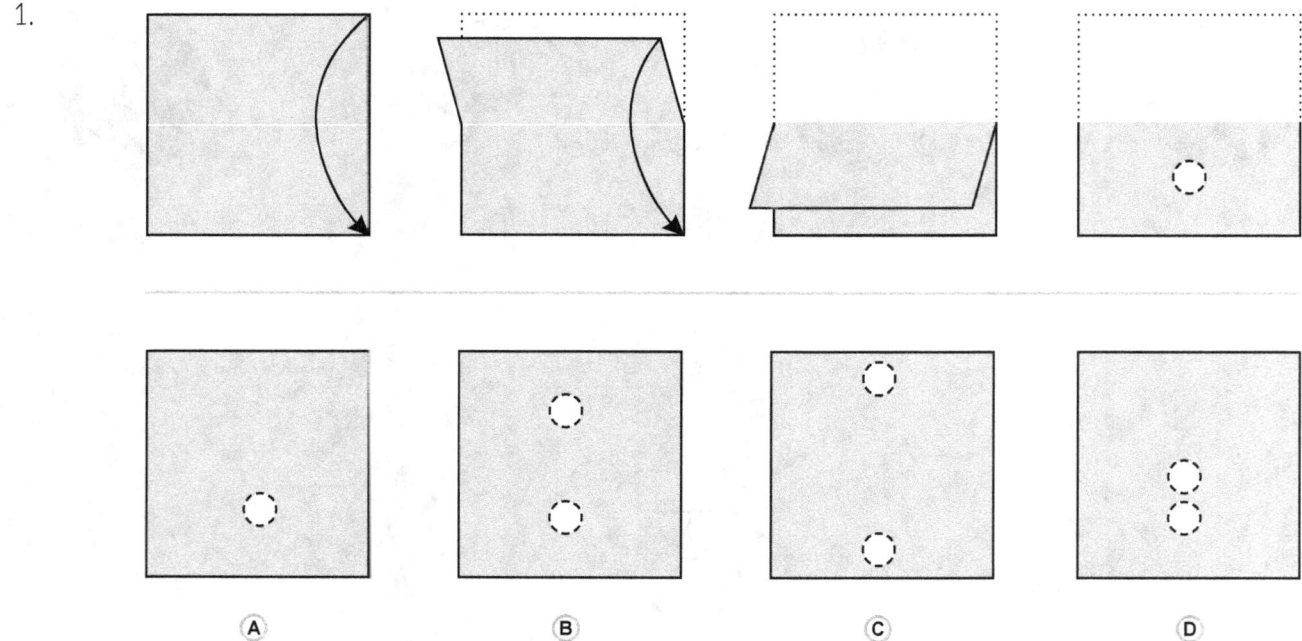

2.

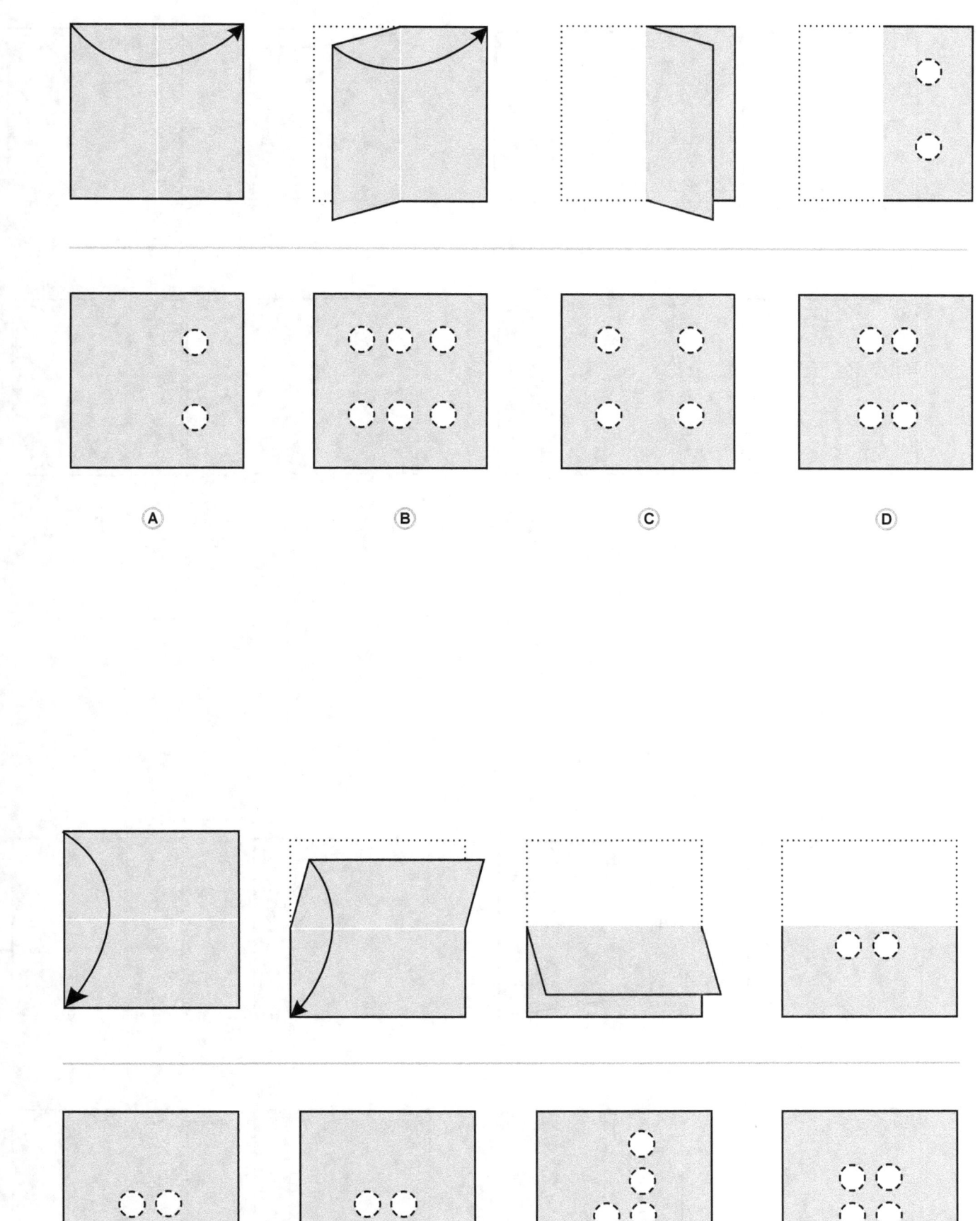

A   B   C   D

3.

A   B   C   D

4.

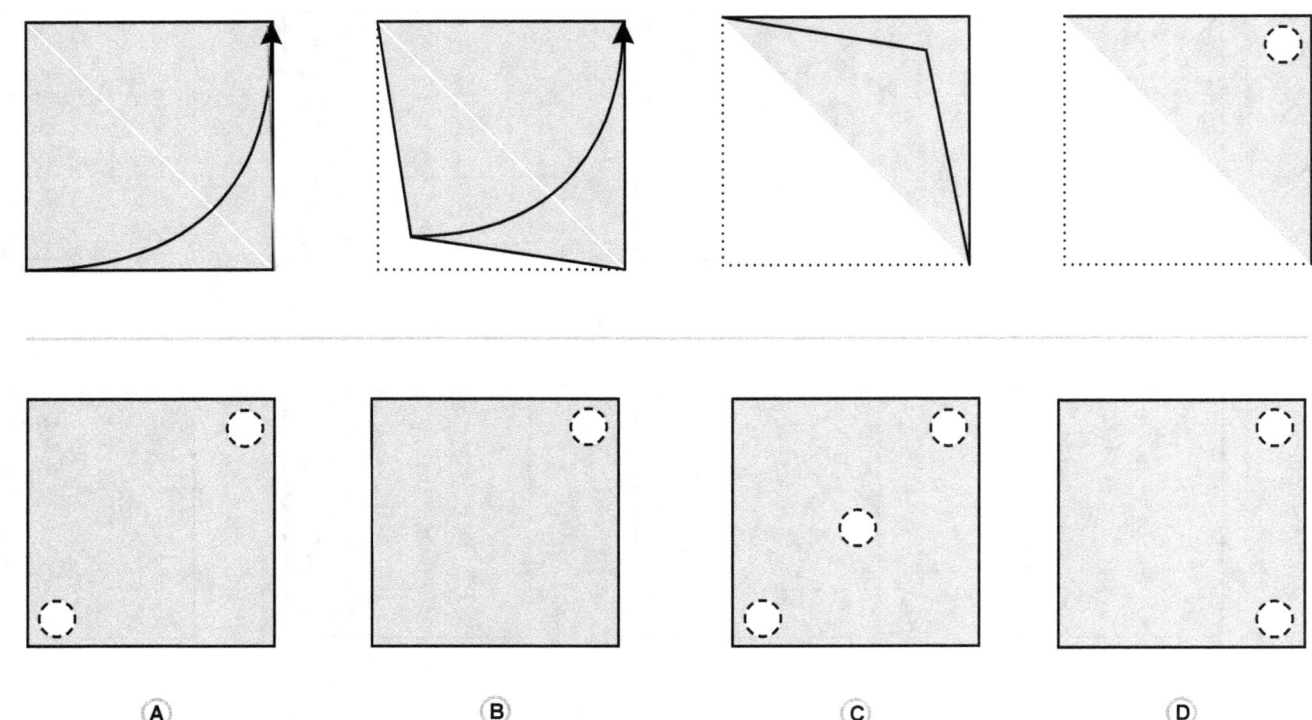

A B C D

5.

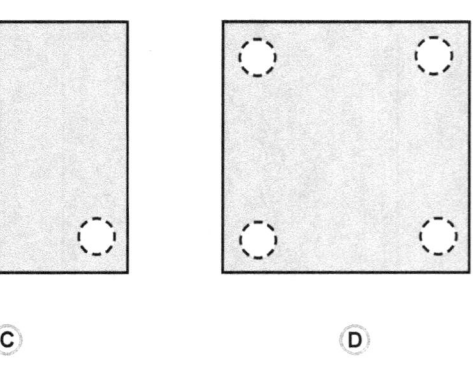

A B C D

6.

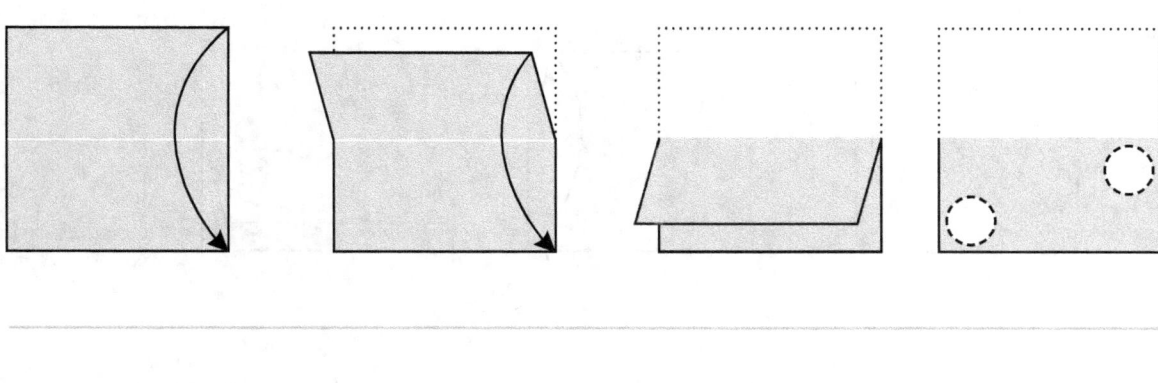

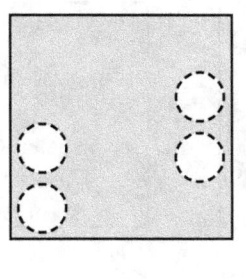
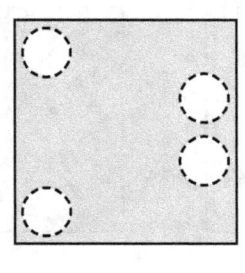
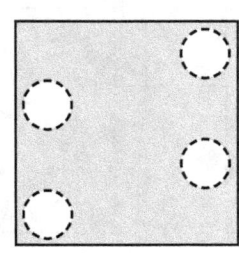
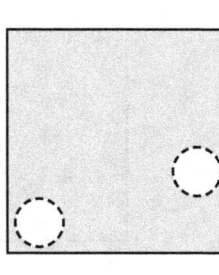

(A) (B) (C) (D)

7.

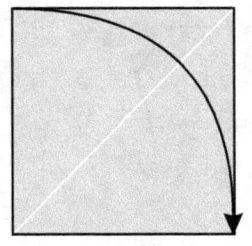
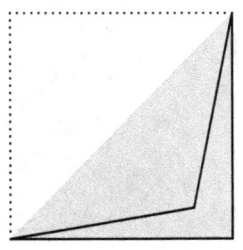
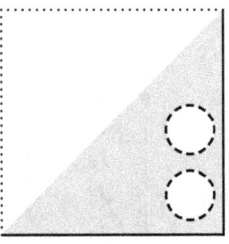

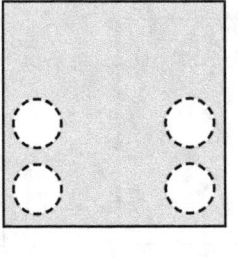
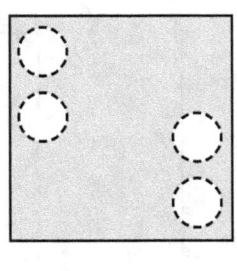
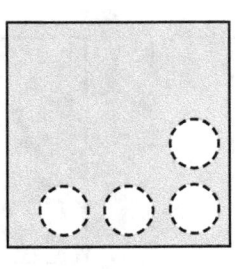
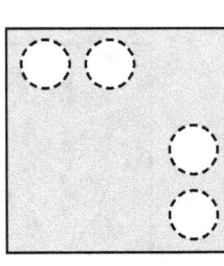

(A) (B) (C) (D)

8.

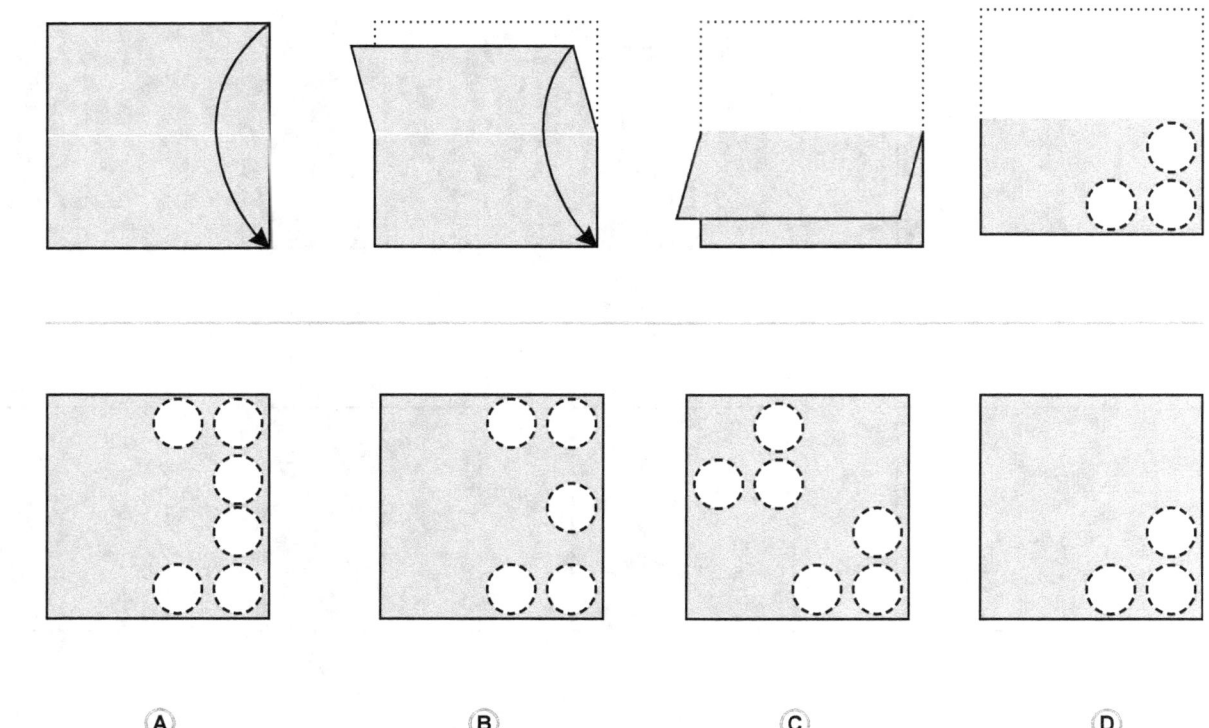

9.

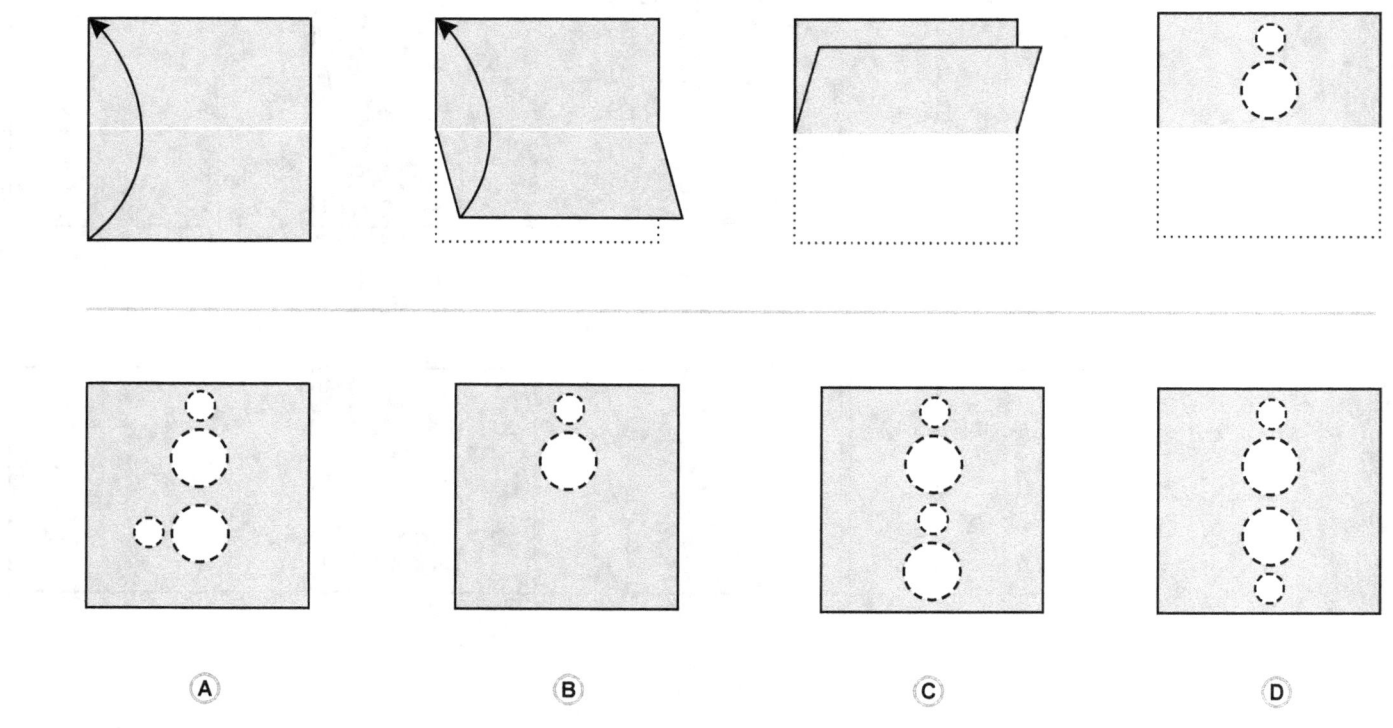

10.

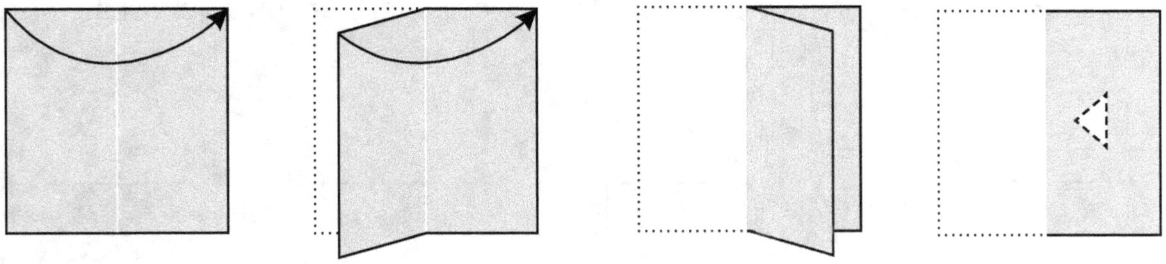

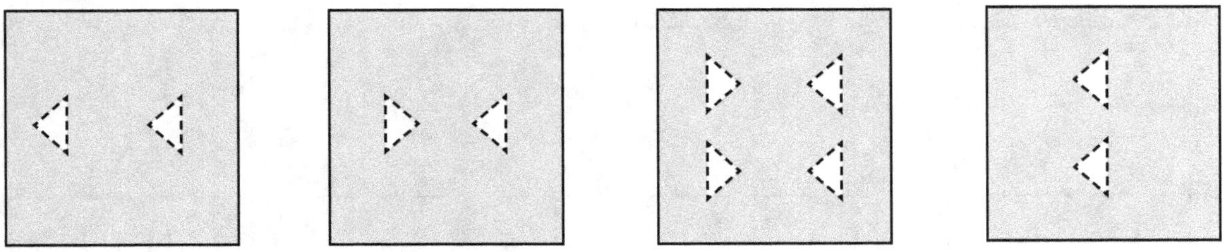

A   B   C   D

11.

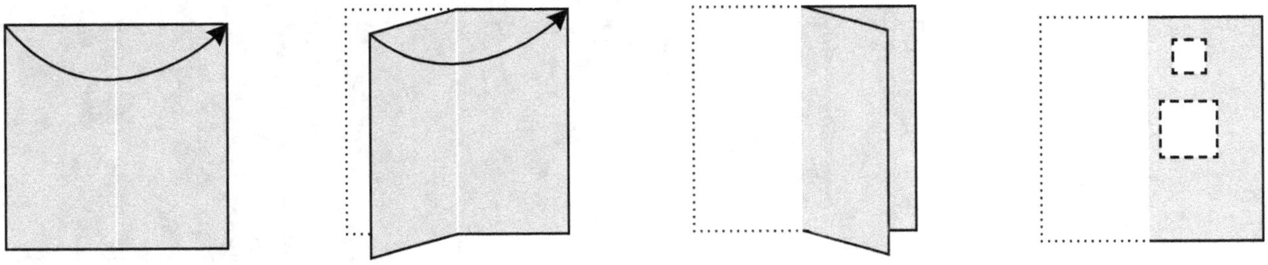

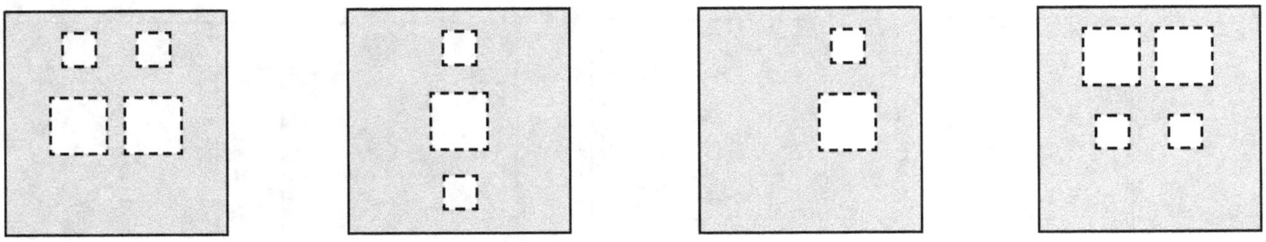

A   B   C   D

Note: In the next four questions, the paper is folded twice. Point this out to your child.

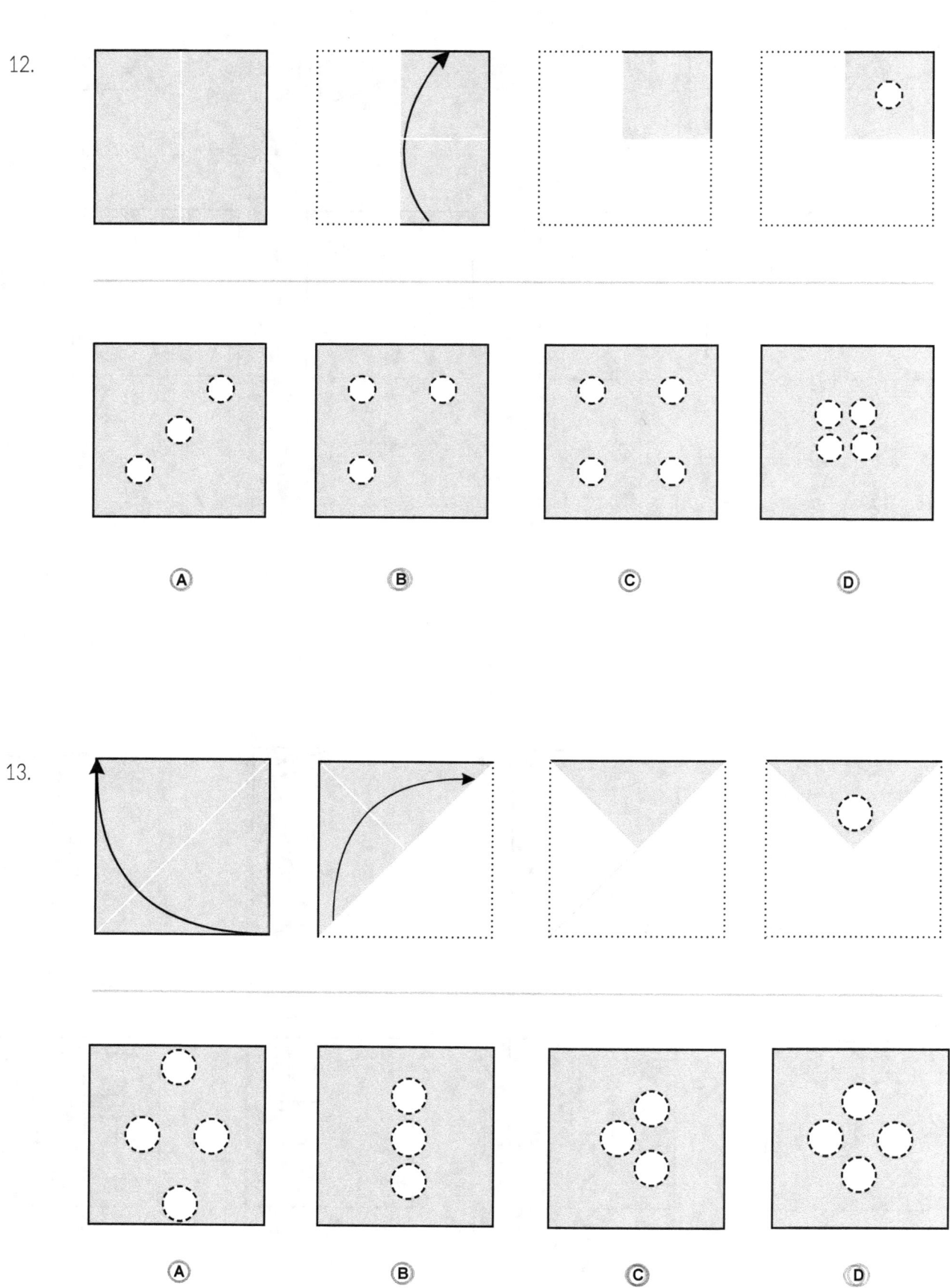

12.

13.

14.

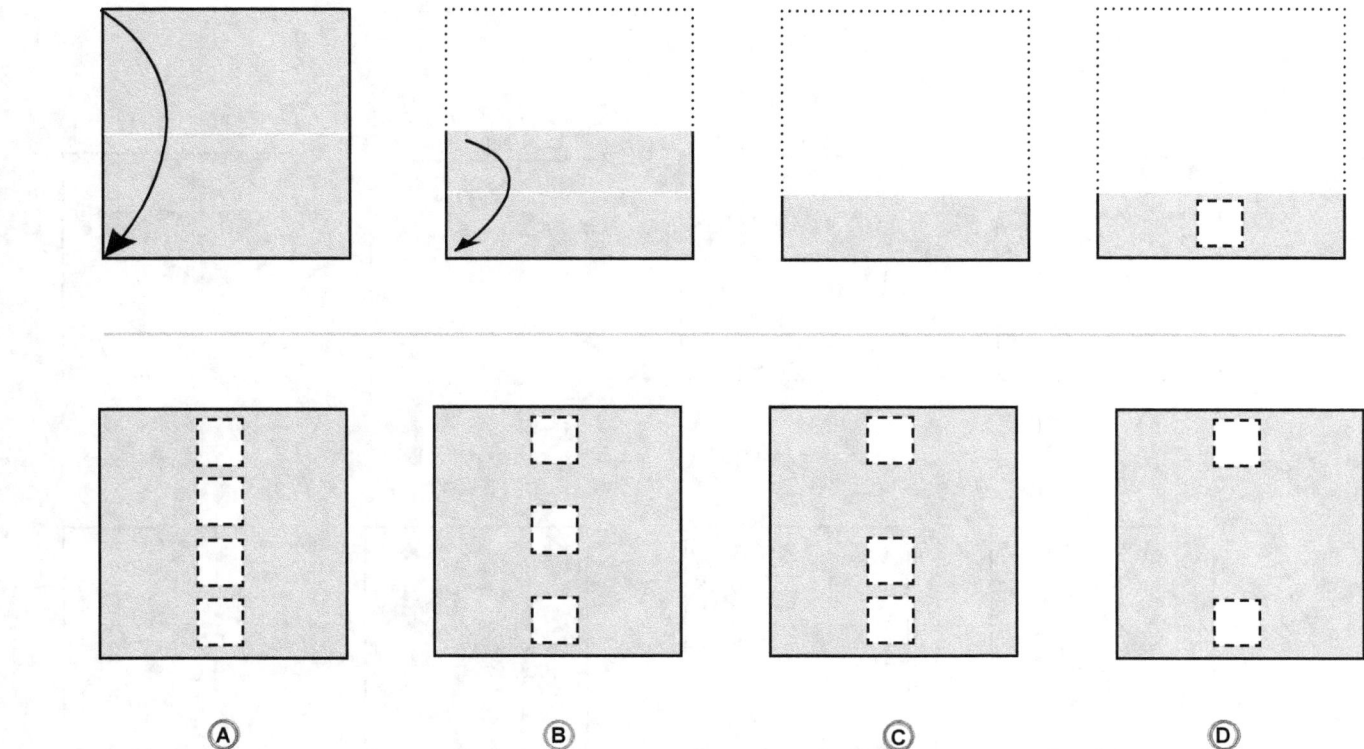

(A)   (B)   (C)   (D)

15.

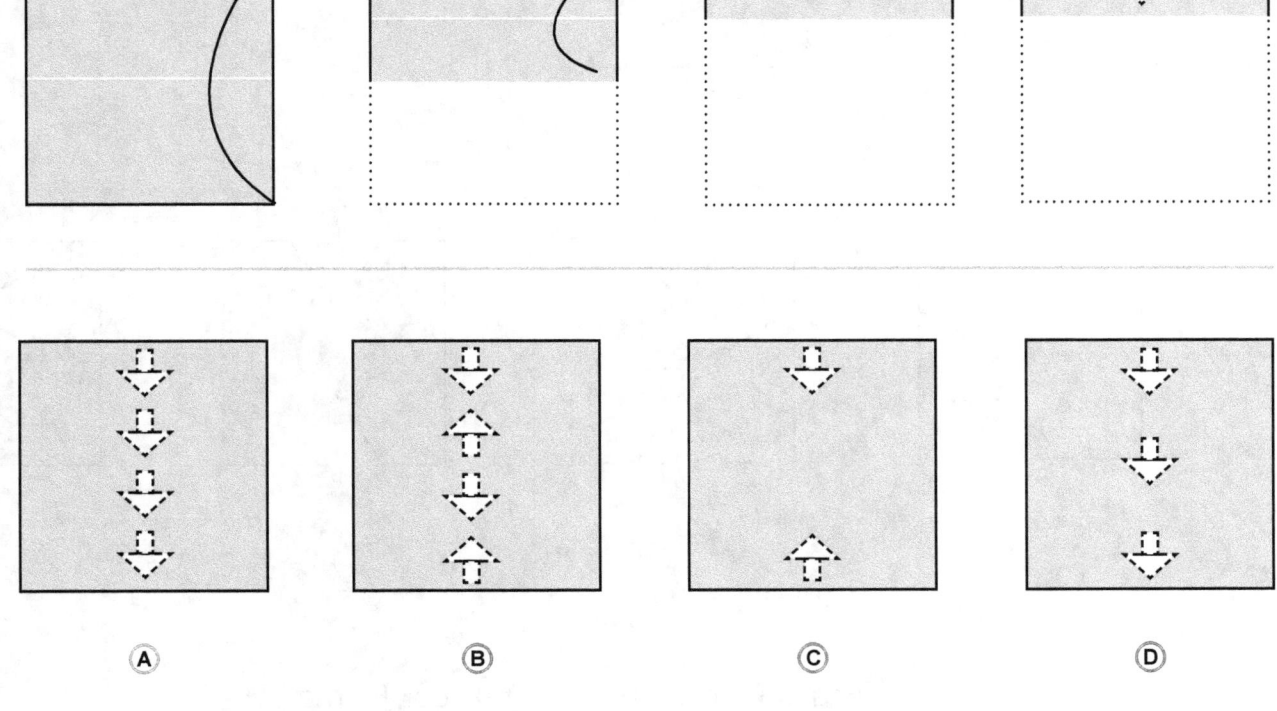

(A)   (B)   (C)   (D)

16.

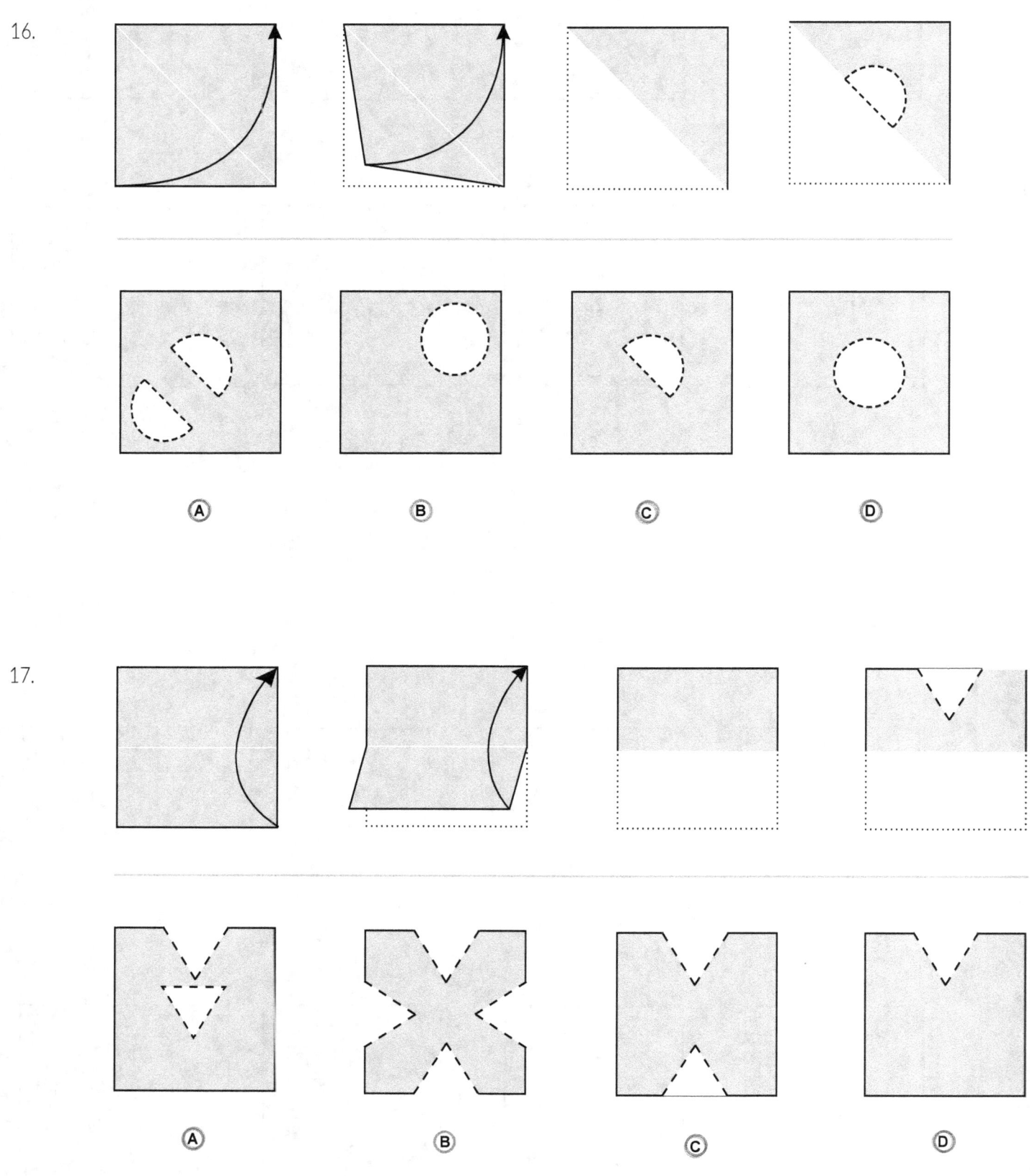

A   B   C   D

17.

A   B   C   D

- End of Practice Test 1 (Workbook Format) -

COGAT® PRACTICE TEST 2

START OF PRACTICE TEST 2 / FIGURE ANALOGIES

Directions: The pictures in the top boxes go together in some way. One of the bottom boxes is empty. Which answer choice goes with the picture in the bottom box in the same way the top pictures do?

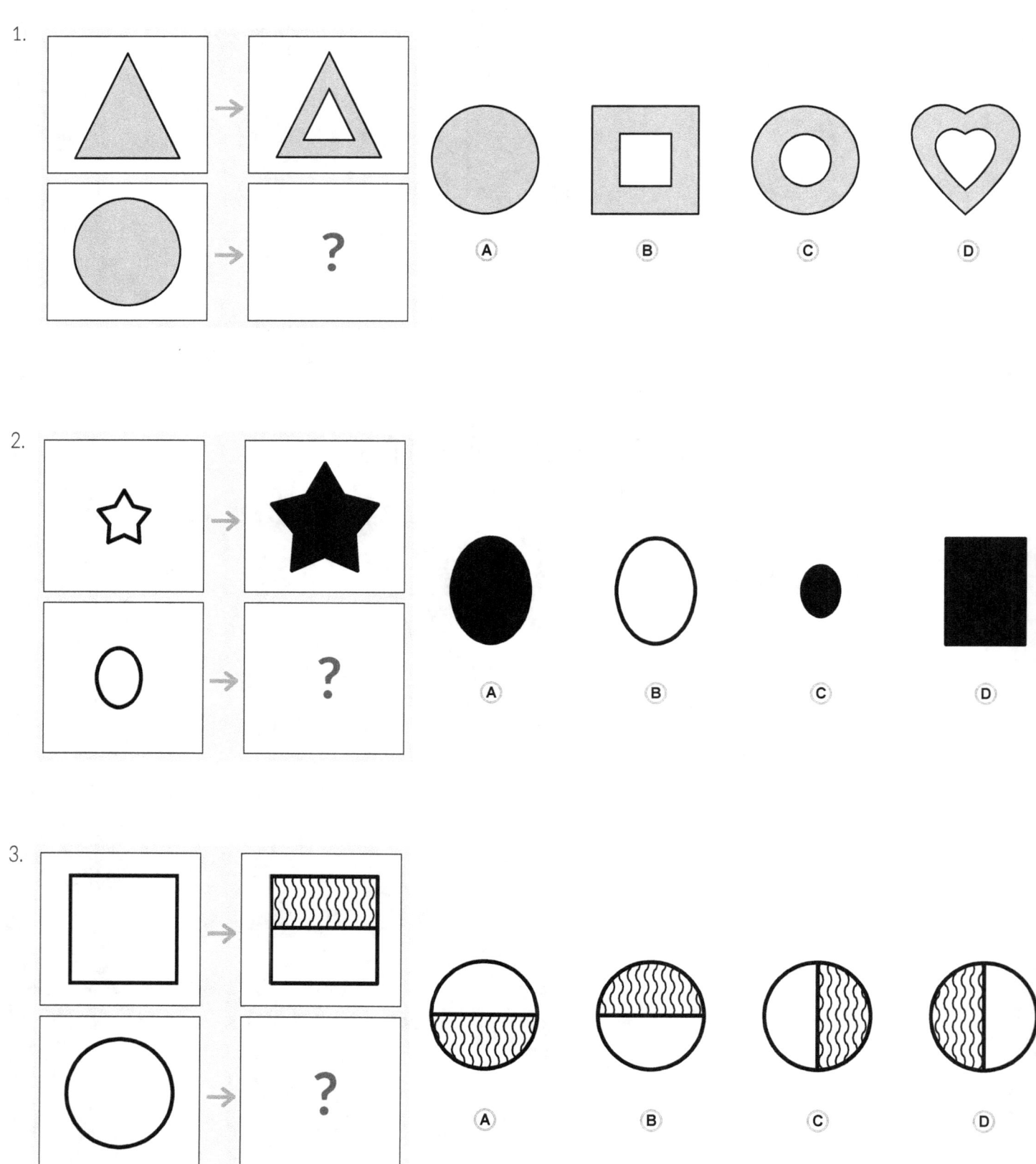

4.

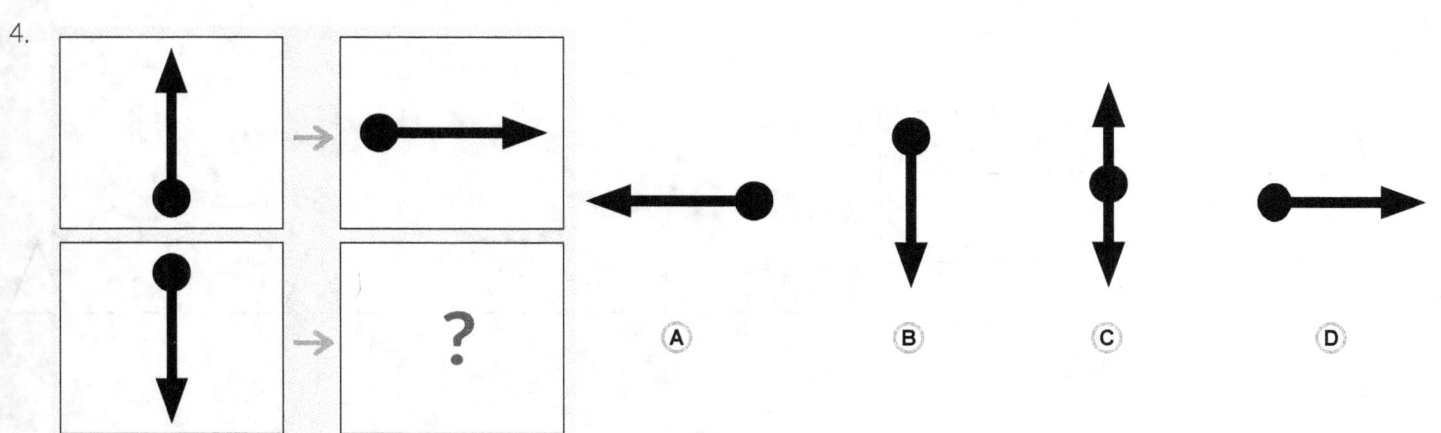

5.

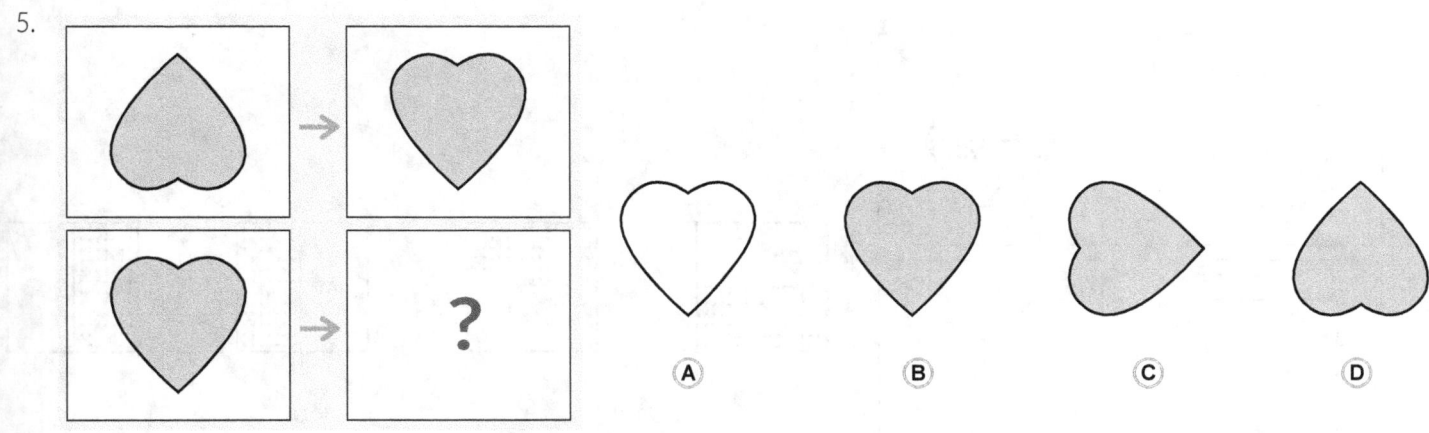

6.

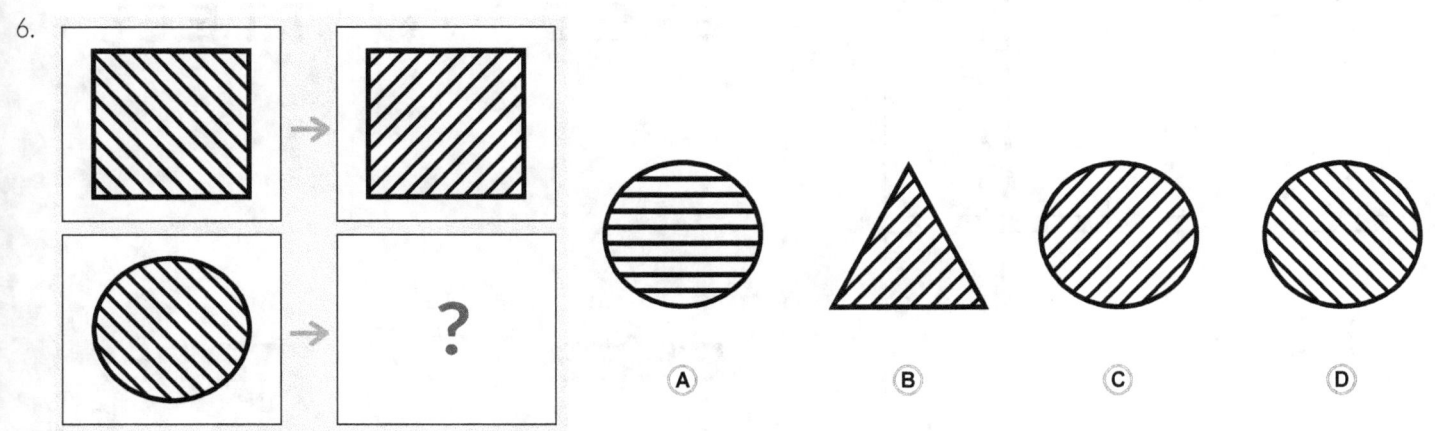

7.

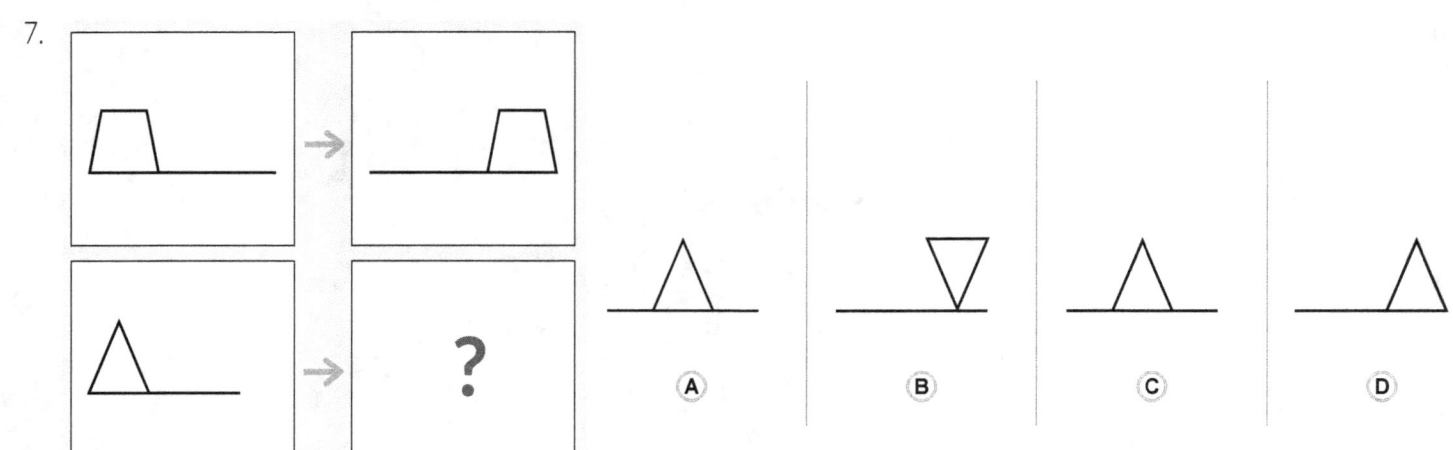

8.

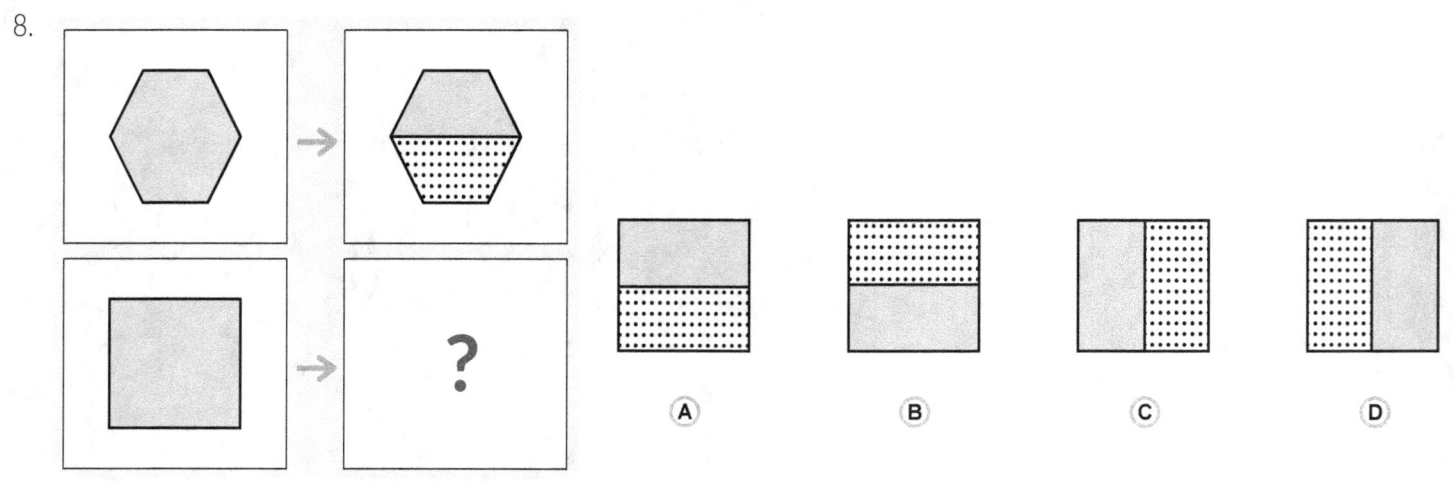

9.

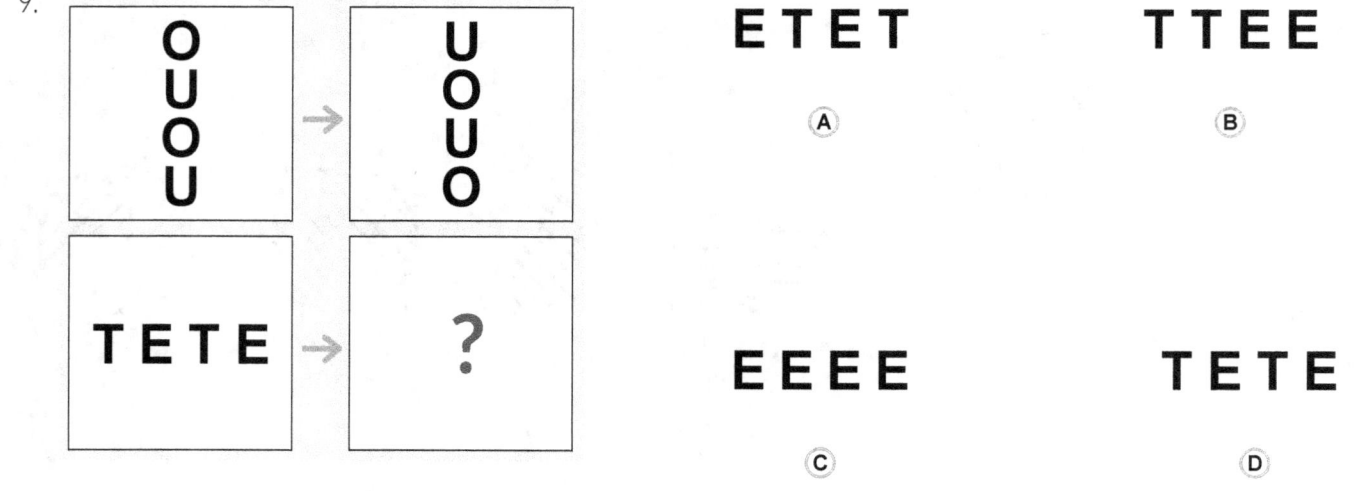

10.

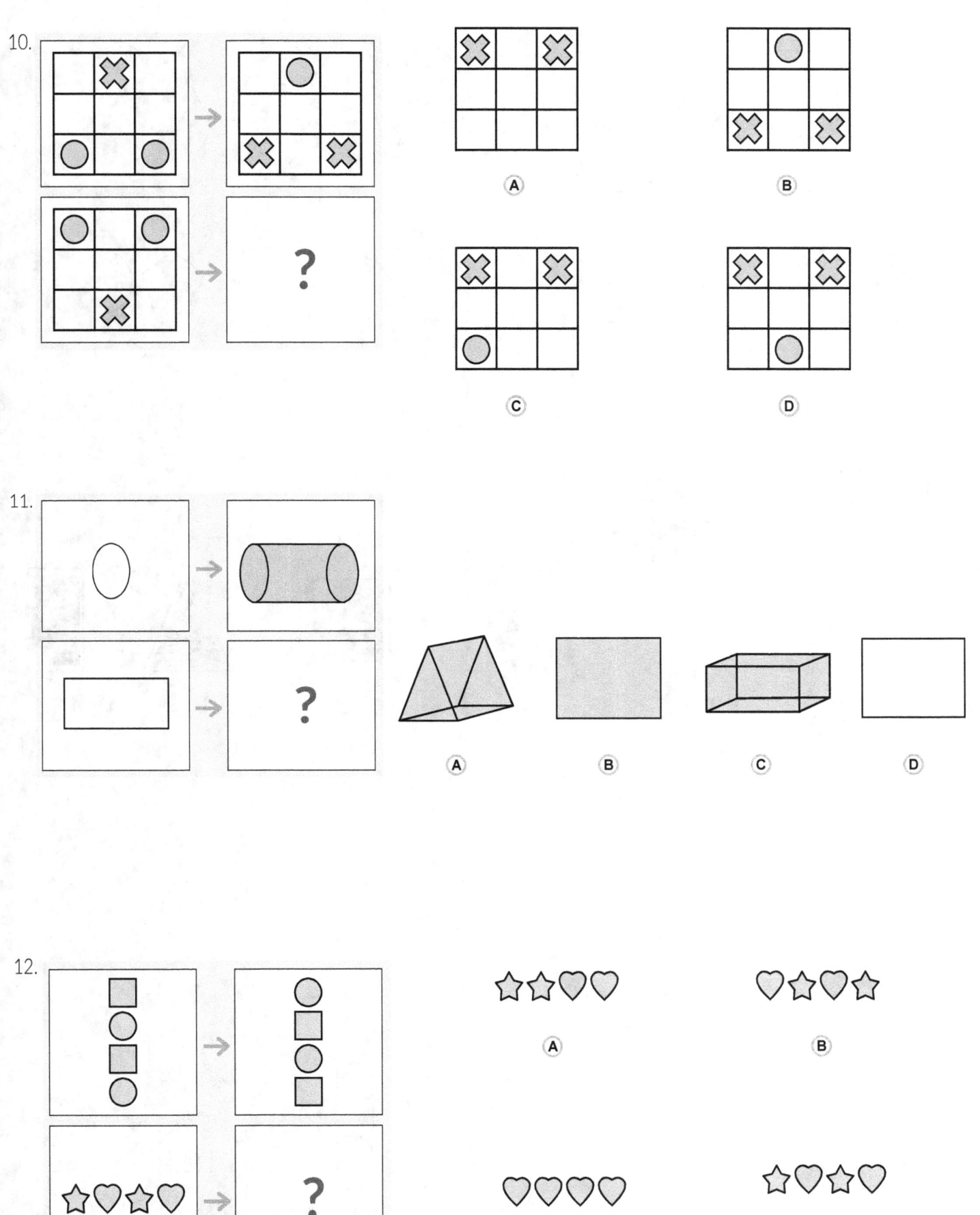

11.

12.

13.

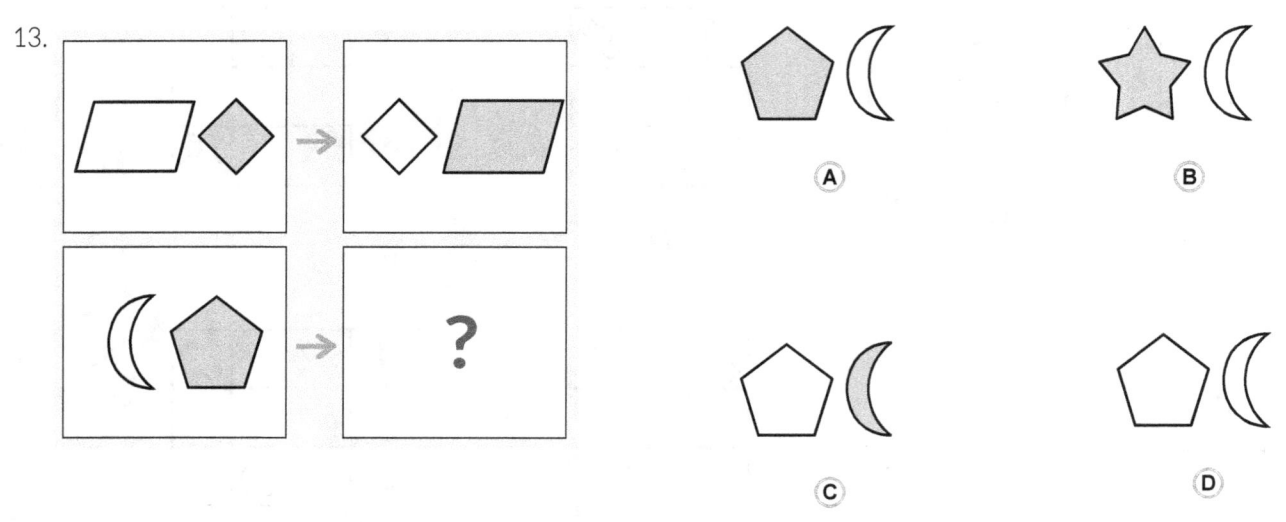

14.

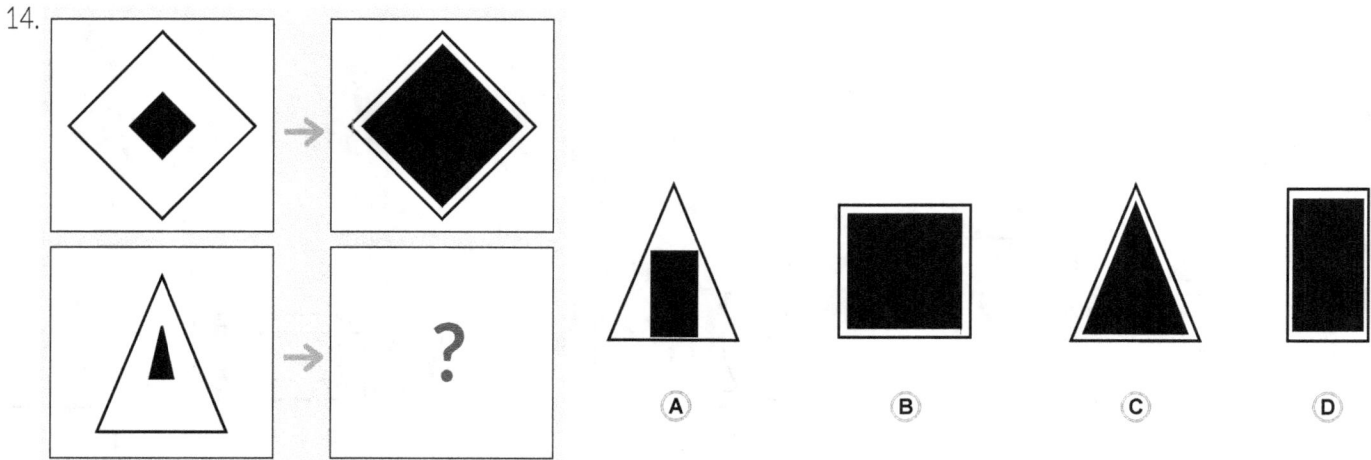

15.

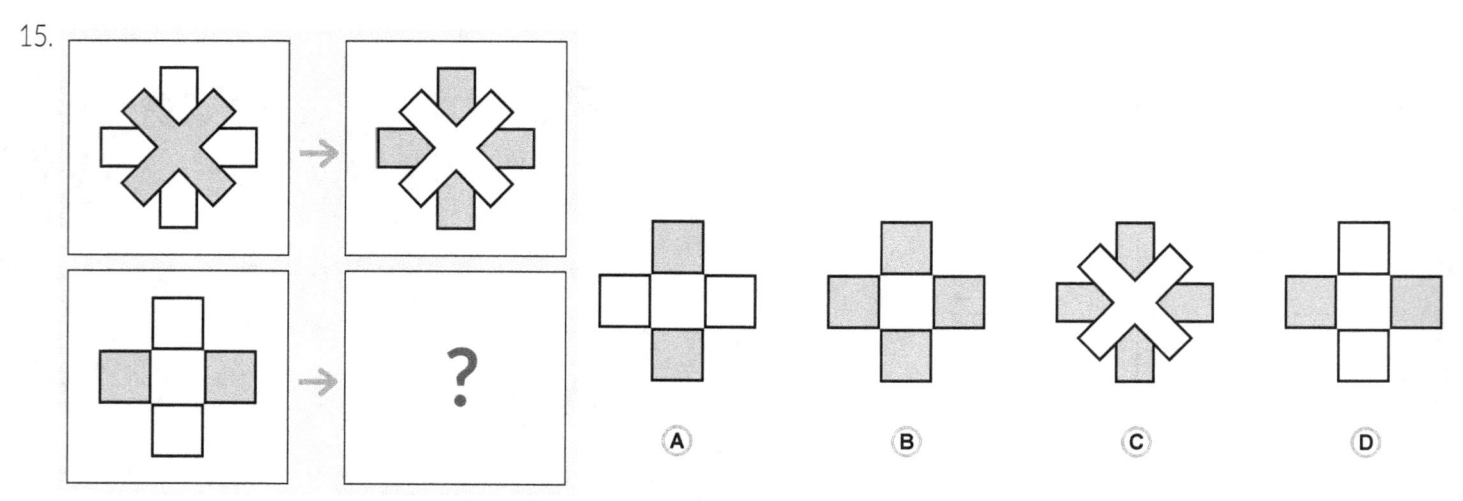

FIGURE CLASSIFICATION

Directions: The top row shows three pictures that are alike in some way. Look at the bottom row. Which bottom picture goes best with the top pictures?

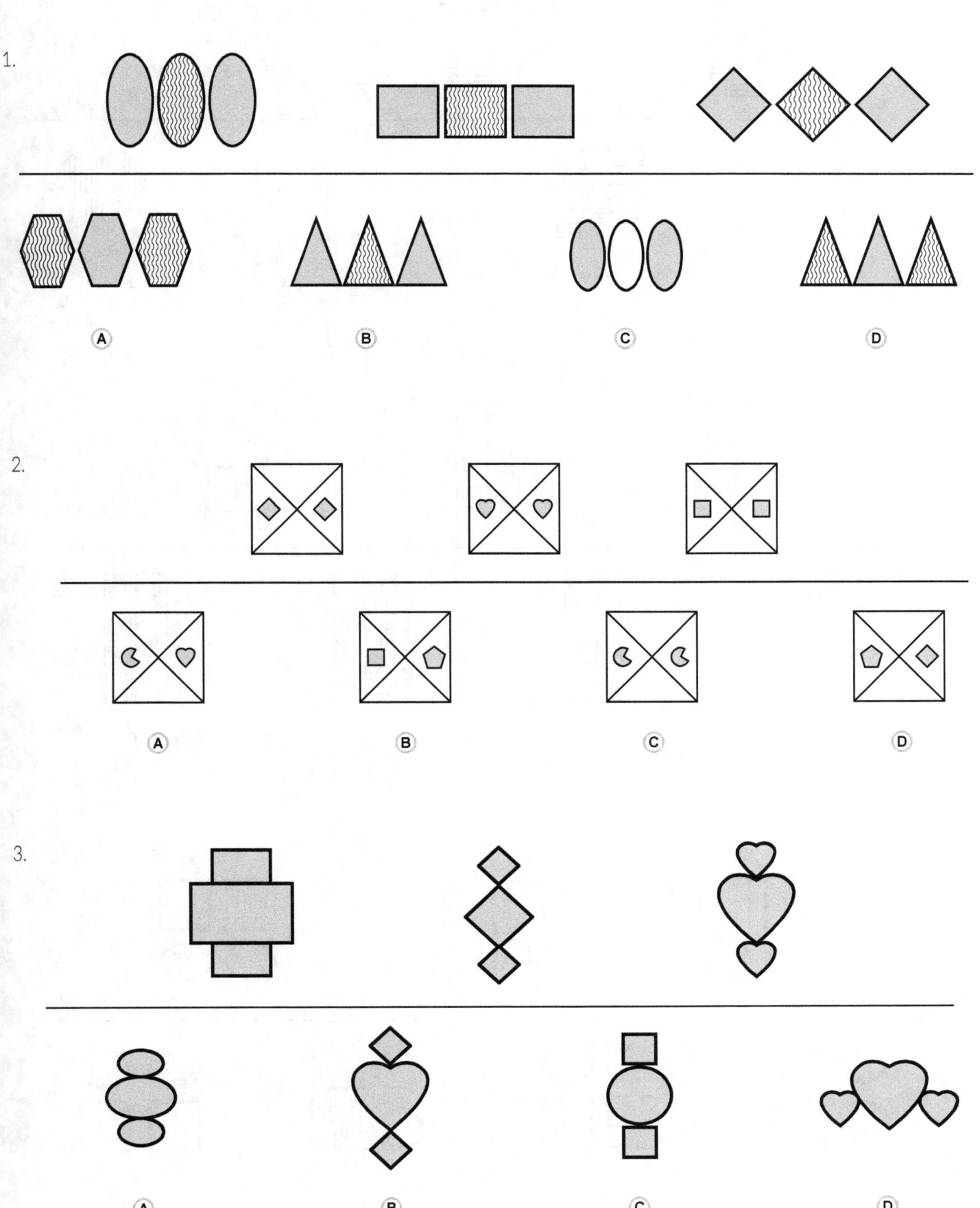

1.

A B C D

2.

A B C D

3.

A B C D

4.

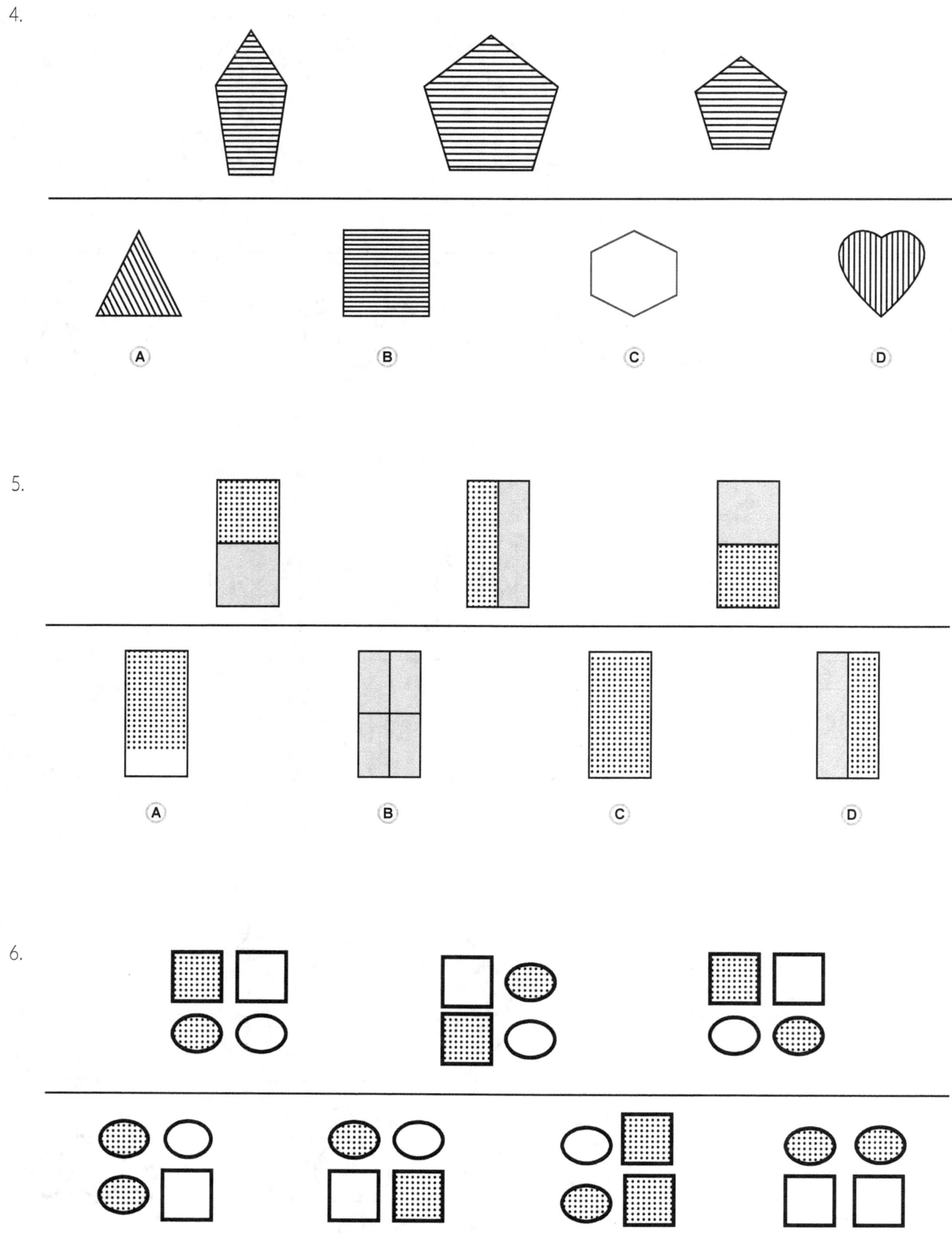

A   B   C   D

5.

A   B   C   D

6.

A   B   C   D

7.

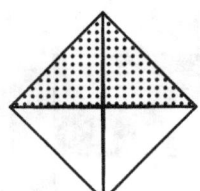 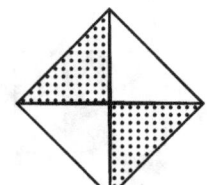 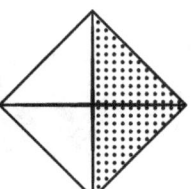

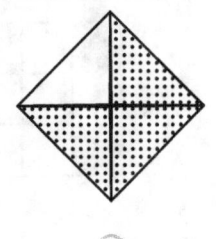 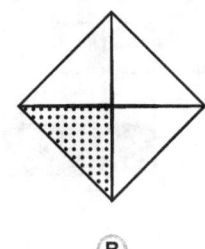 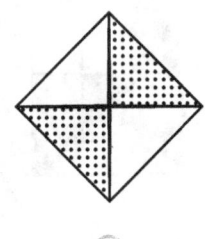 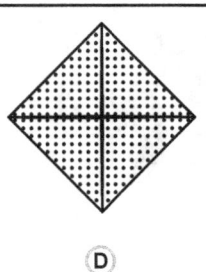

Ⓐ Ⓑ Ⓒ Ⓓ

8.

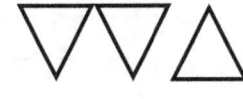 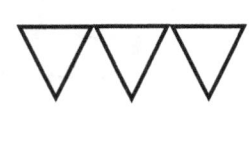

Ⓐ Ⓑ Ⓒ Ⓓ

9.

  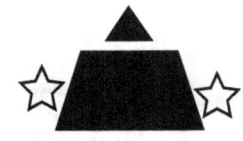

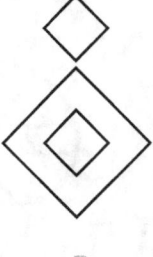   

Ⓐ Ⓑ Ⓒ Ⓓ

10.

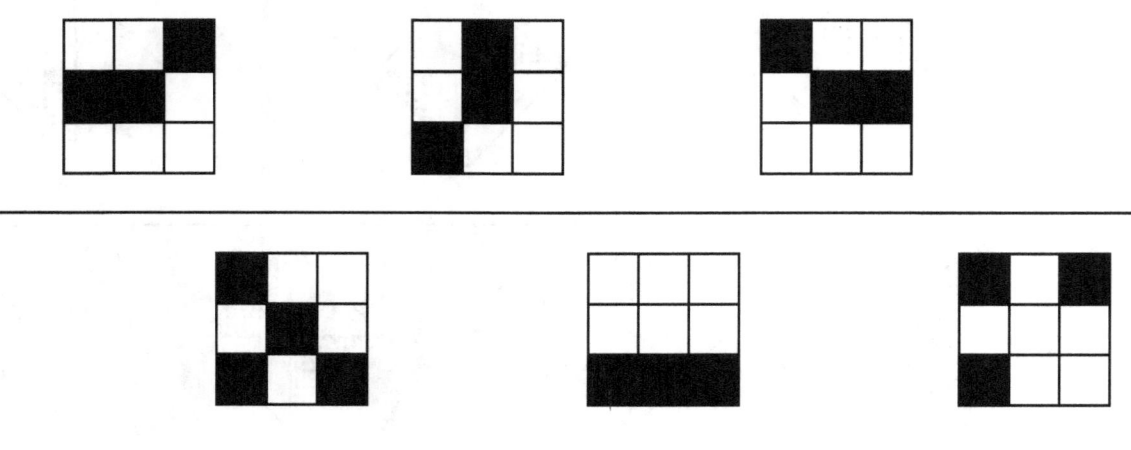

11.

12.

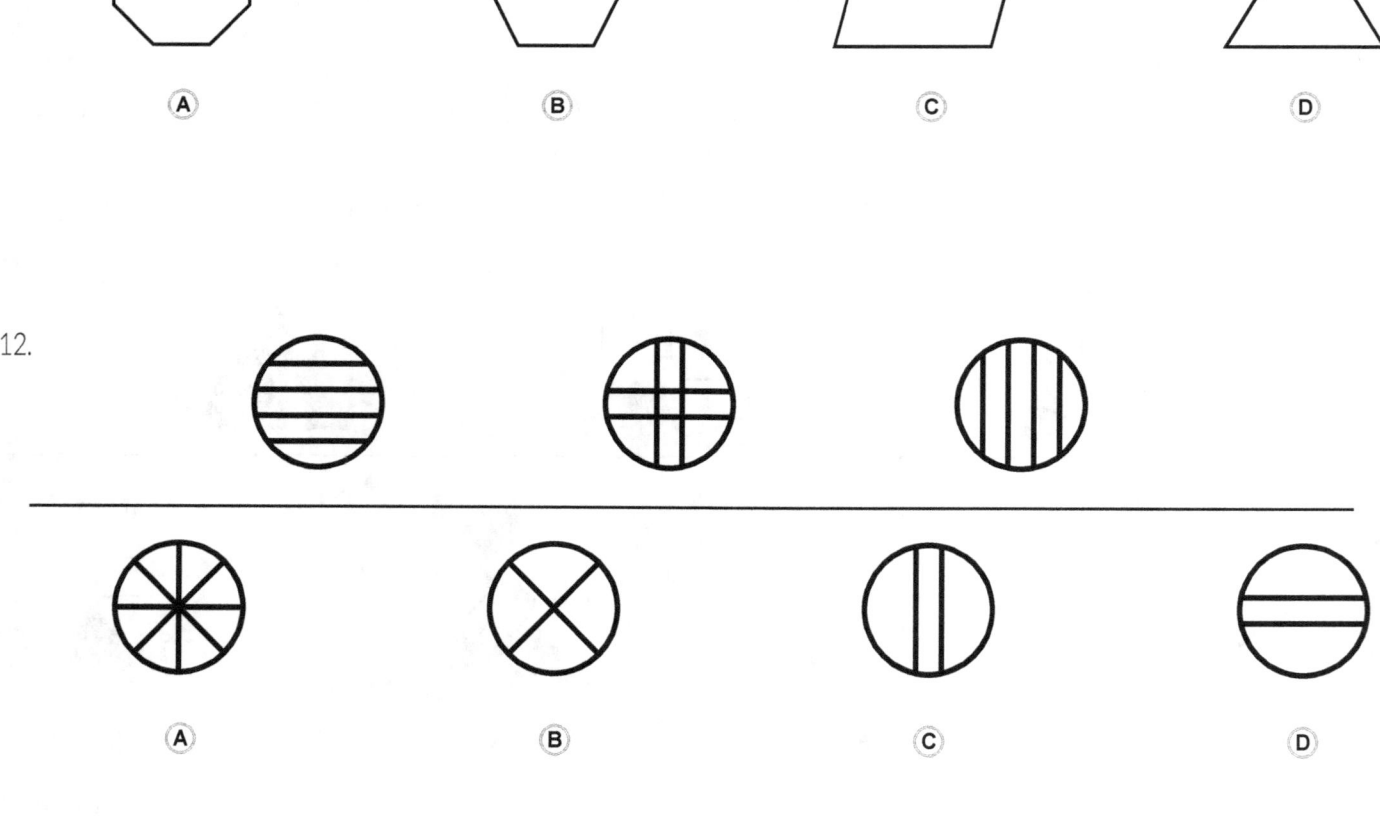

13.

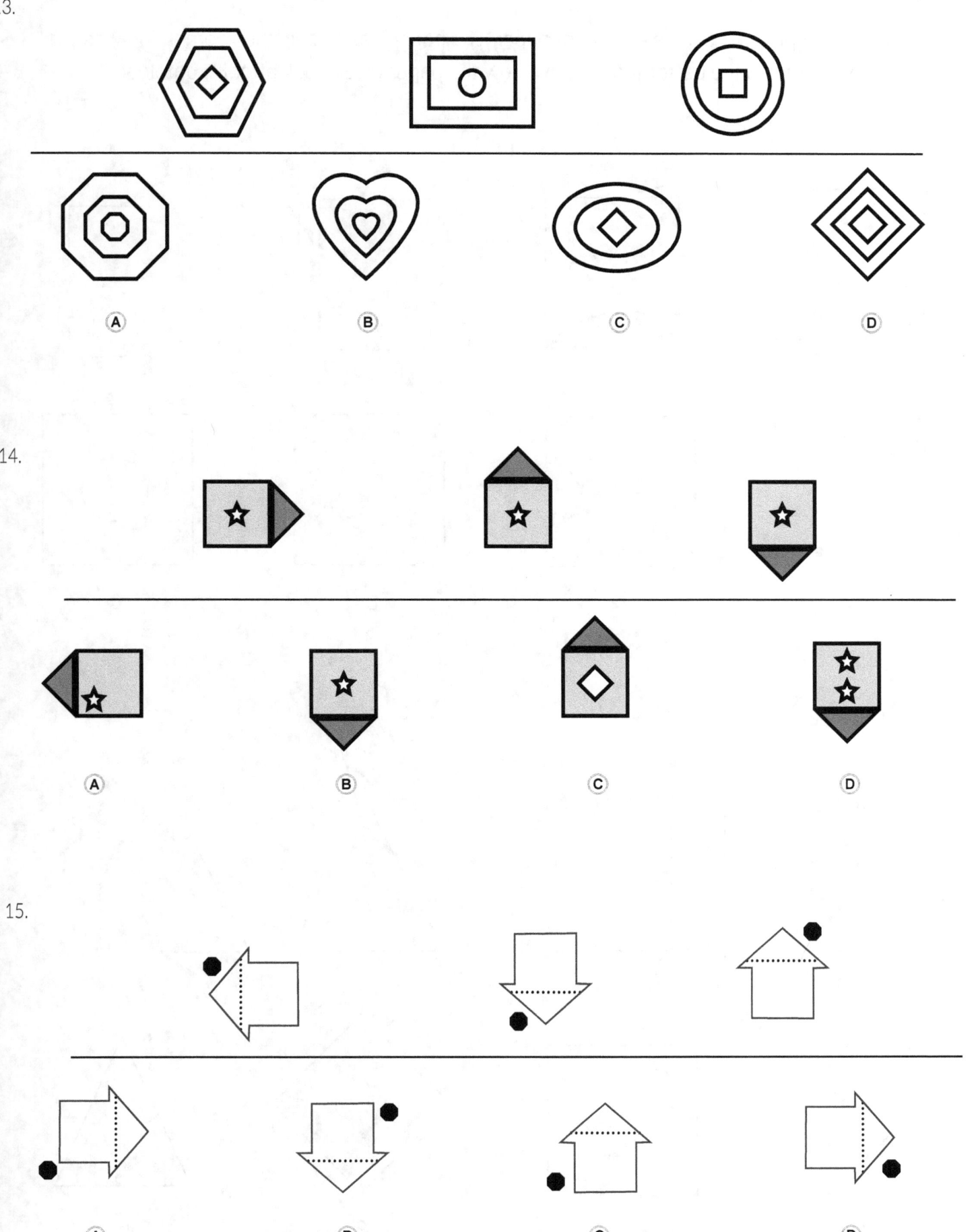

14.

15.

PAPER FOLDING

The top row of pictures shows a sheet of paper. The paper was folded, then something was cut out. Which picture in the bottom row shows how the paper would look after it's unfolded?

1.

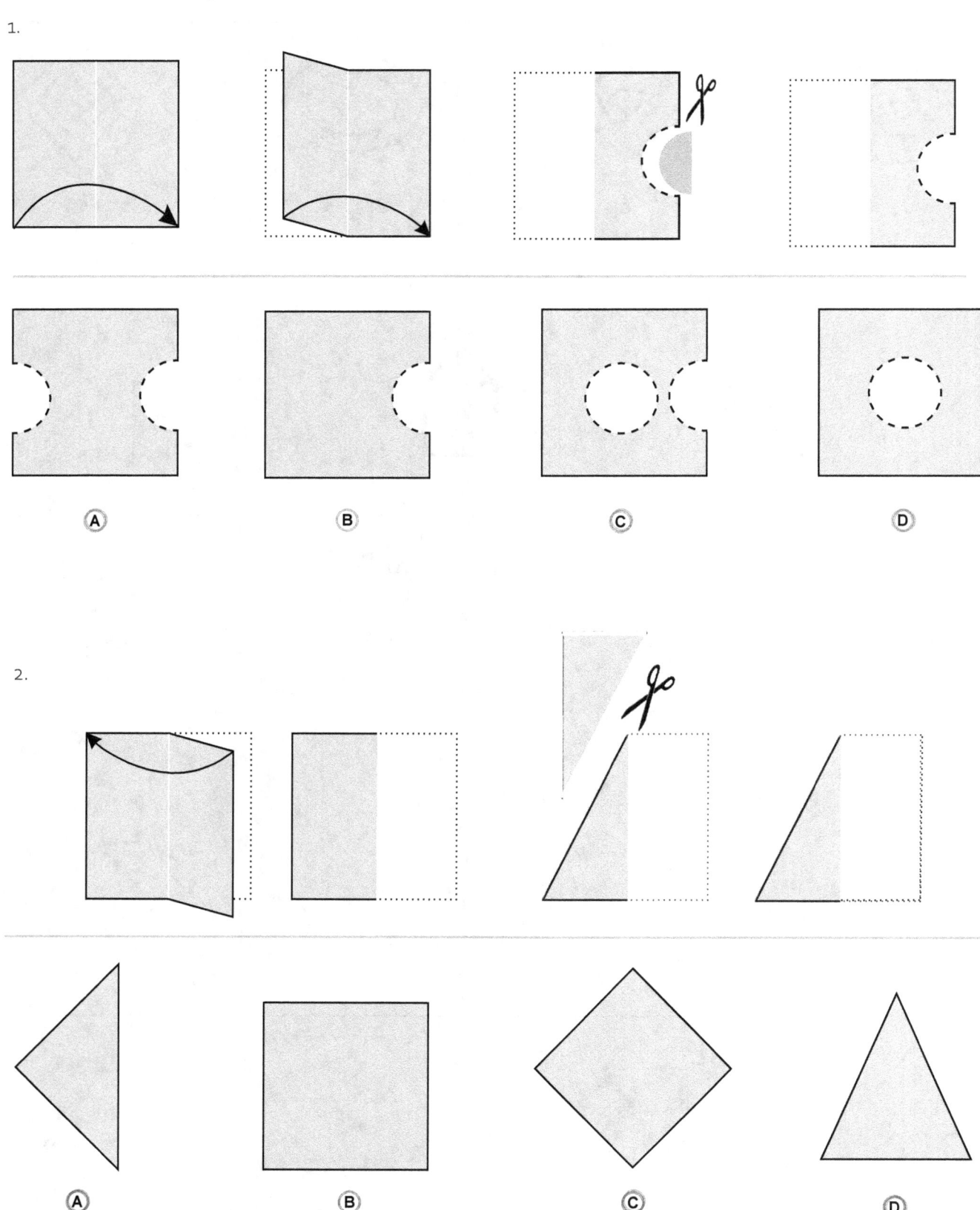

3.

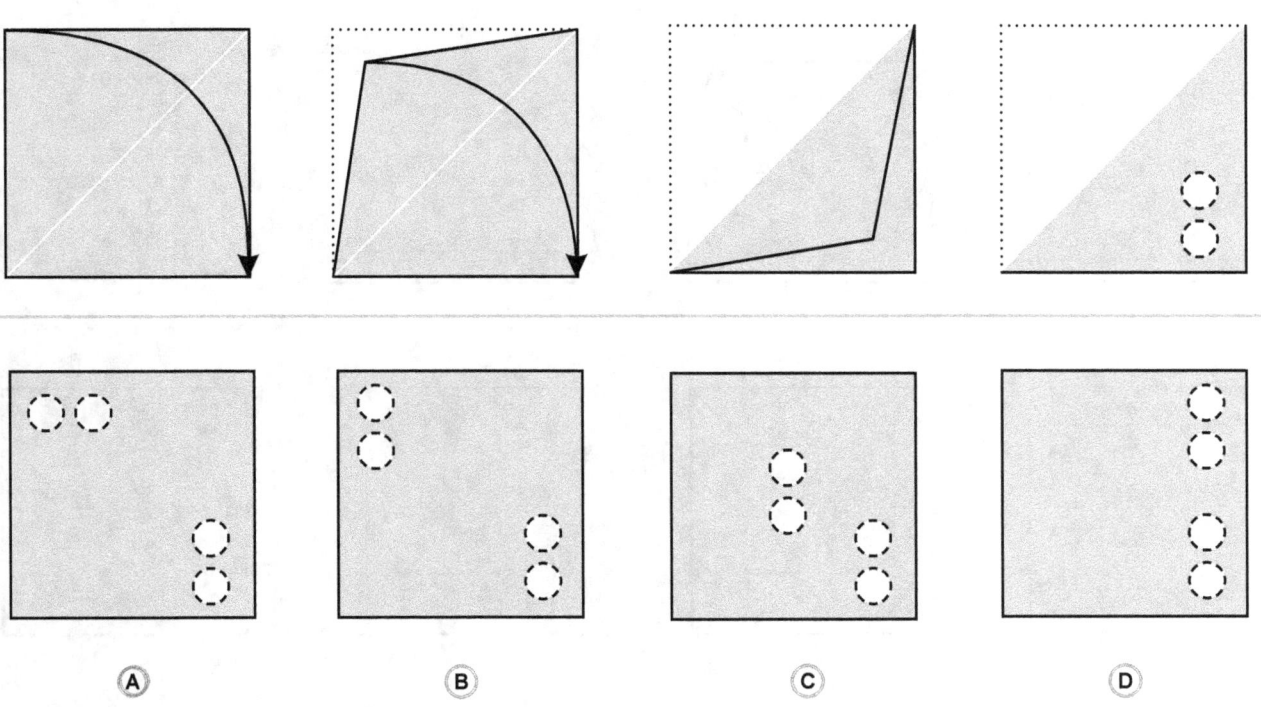

4.

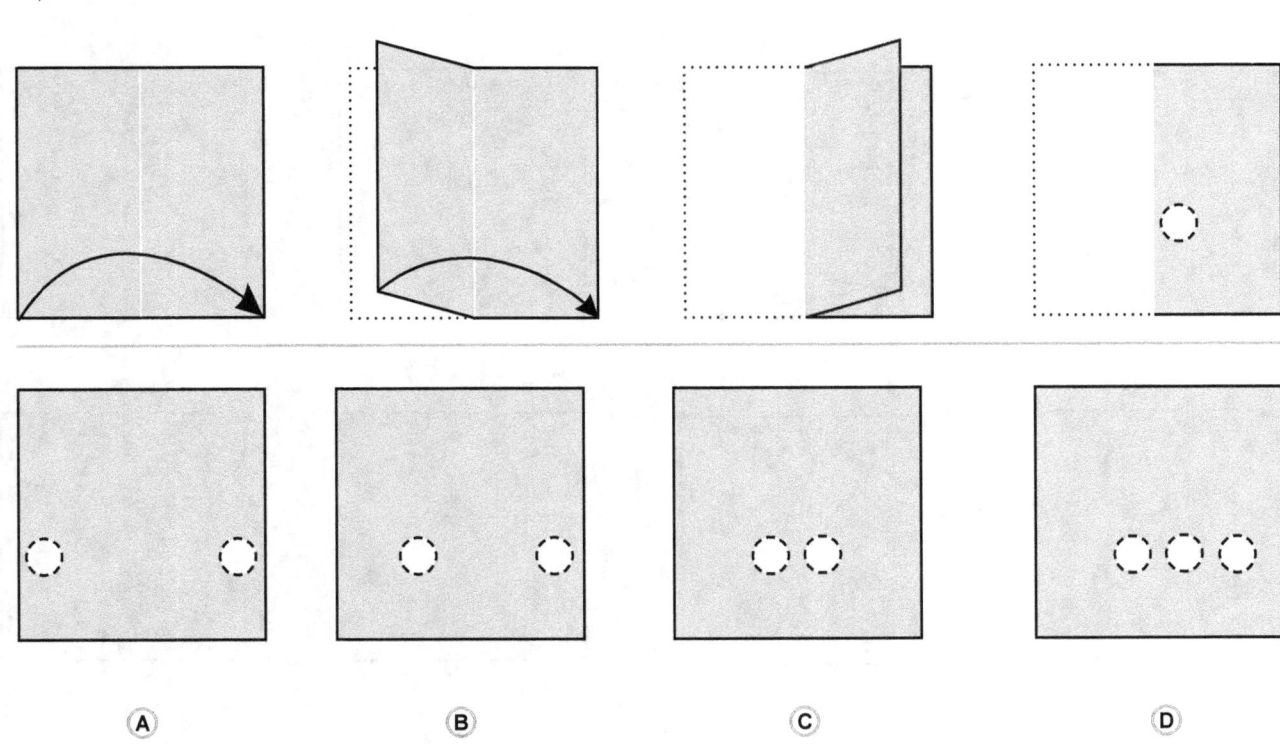

5.

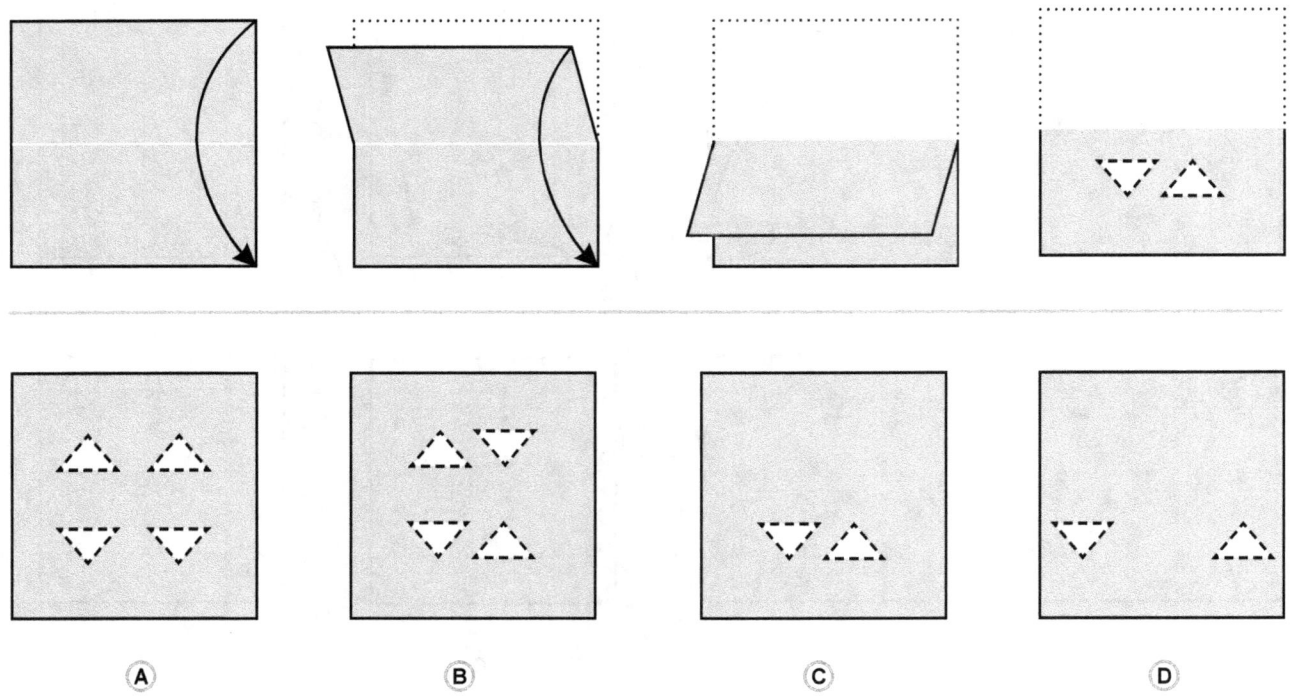

6.

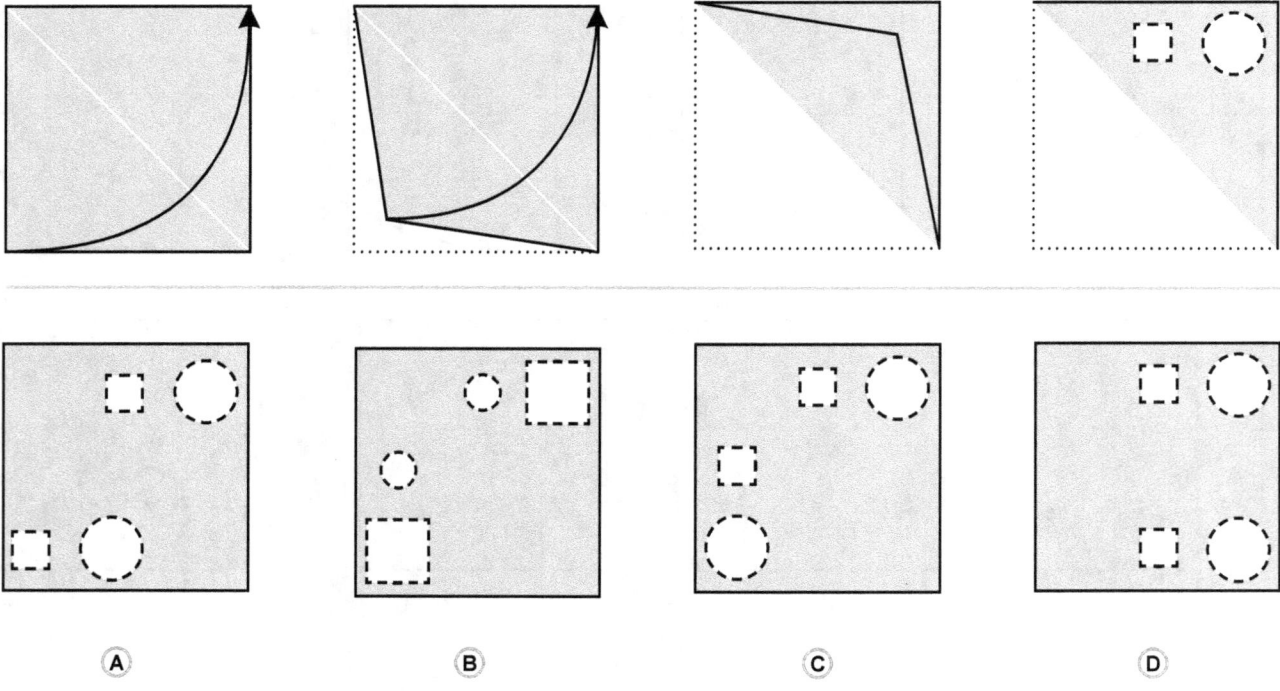

48

7.

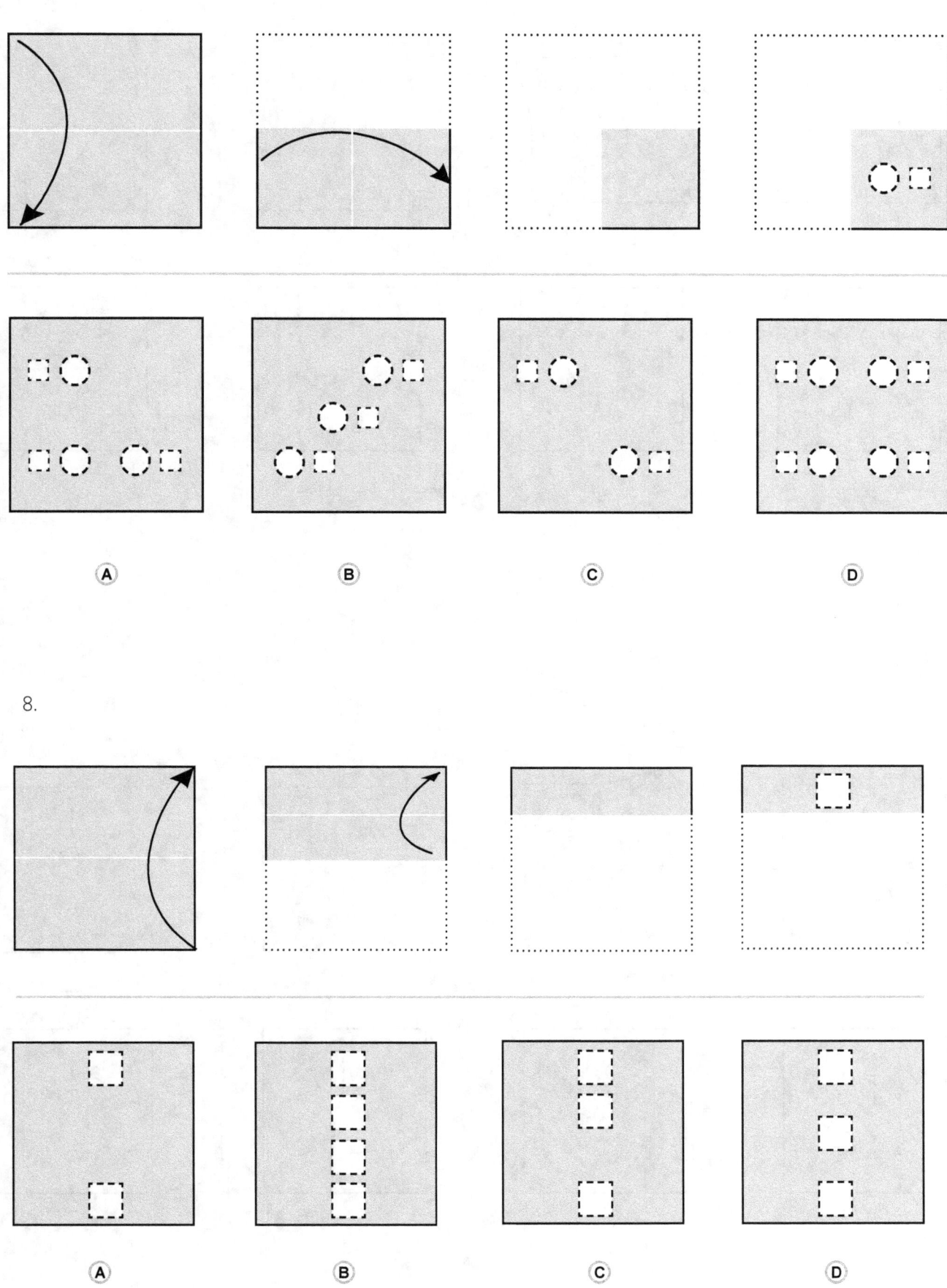

A   B   C   D

8.

A   B   C   D

9.

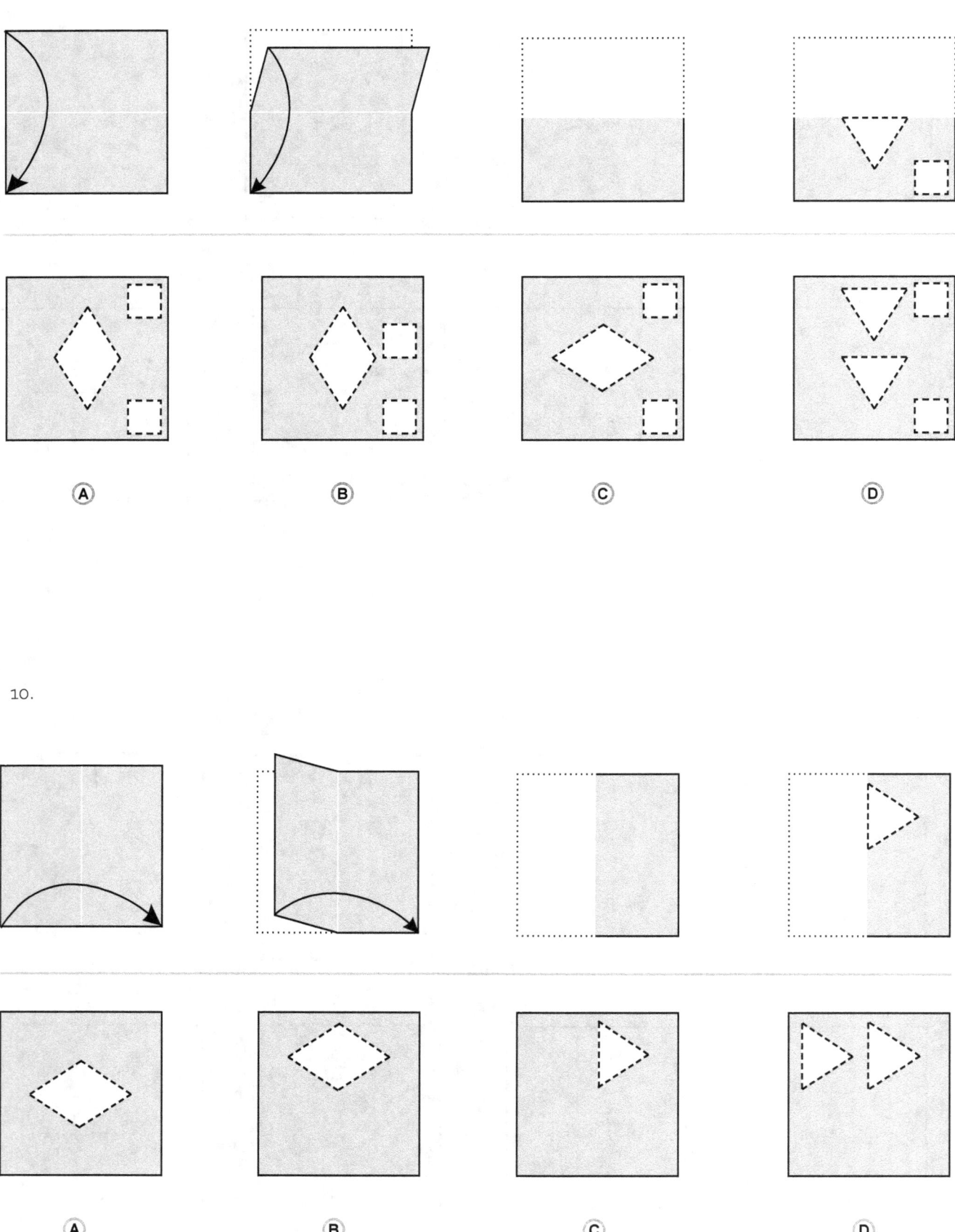

A   B   C   D

10.

A   B   C   D

11.

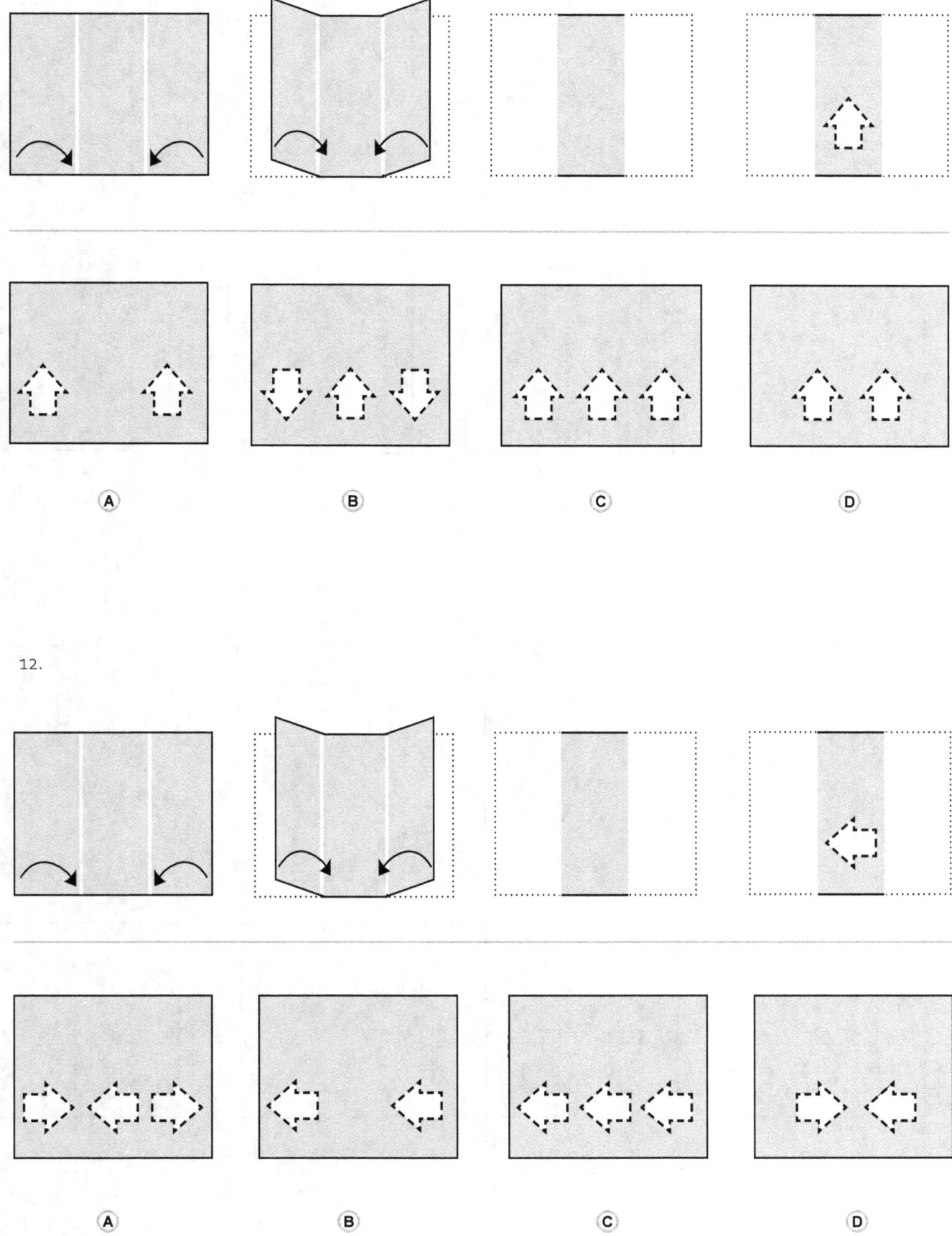

A   B   C   D

12.

A   B   C   D

13.

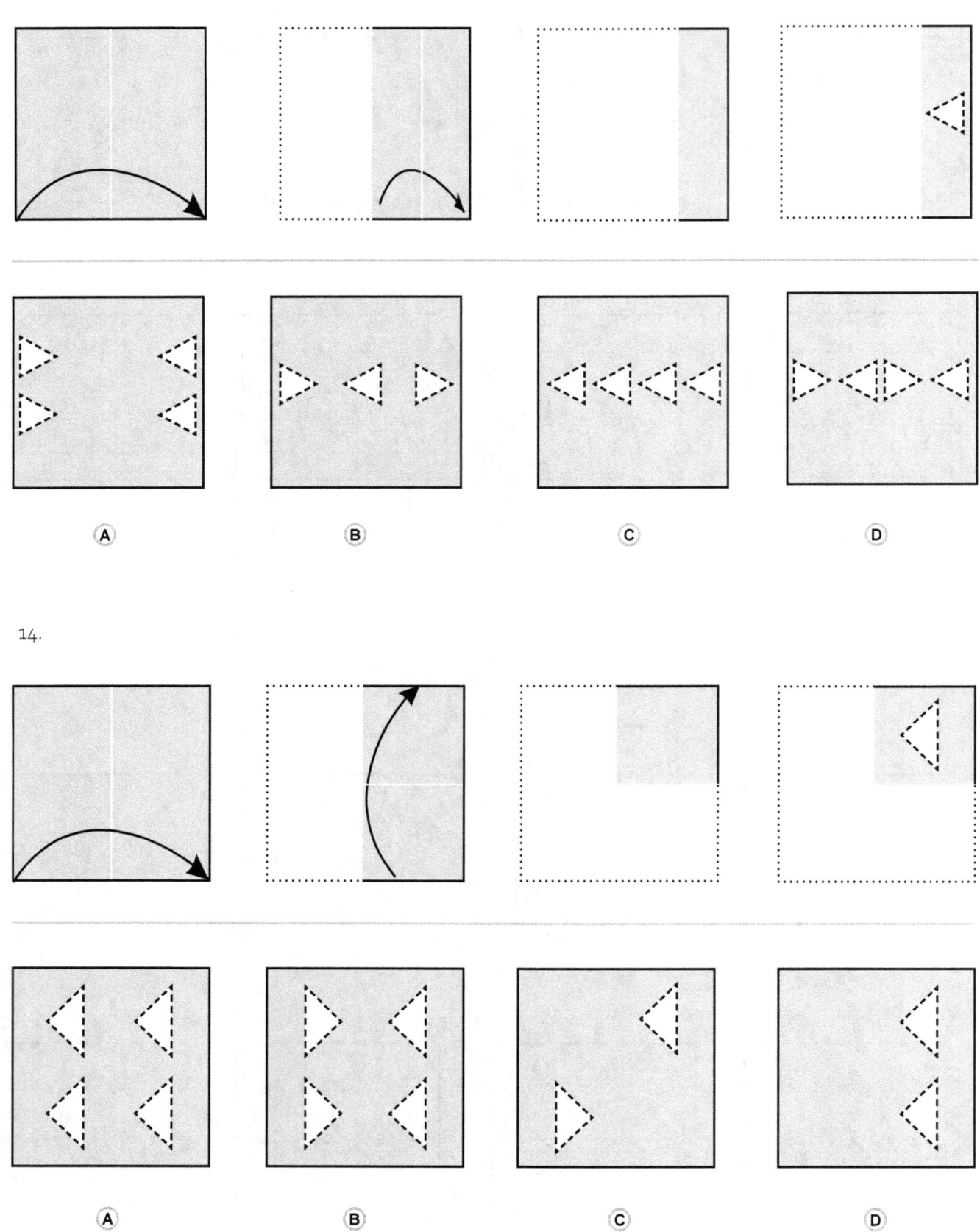

A   B   C   D

14.

A   B   C   D

- End of Practice Test 2 -

COGAT® PRACTICE TEST 3

Directions: The pictures in the top boxes go together in some way. One of the bottom boxes is empty. Which answer choice goes with the picture in the bottom box in the same way the top pictures do?

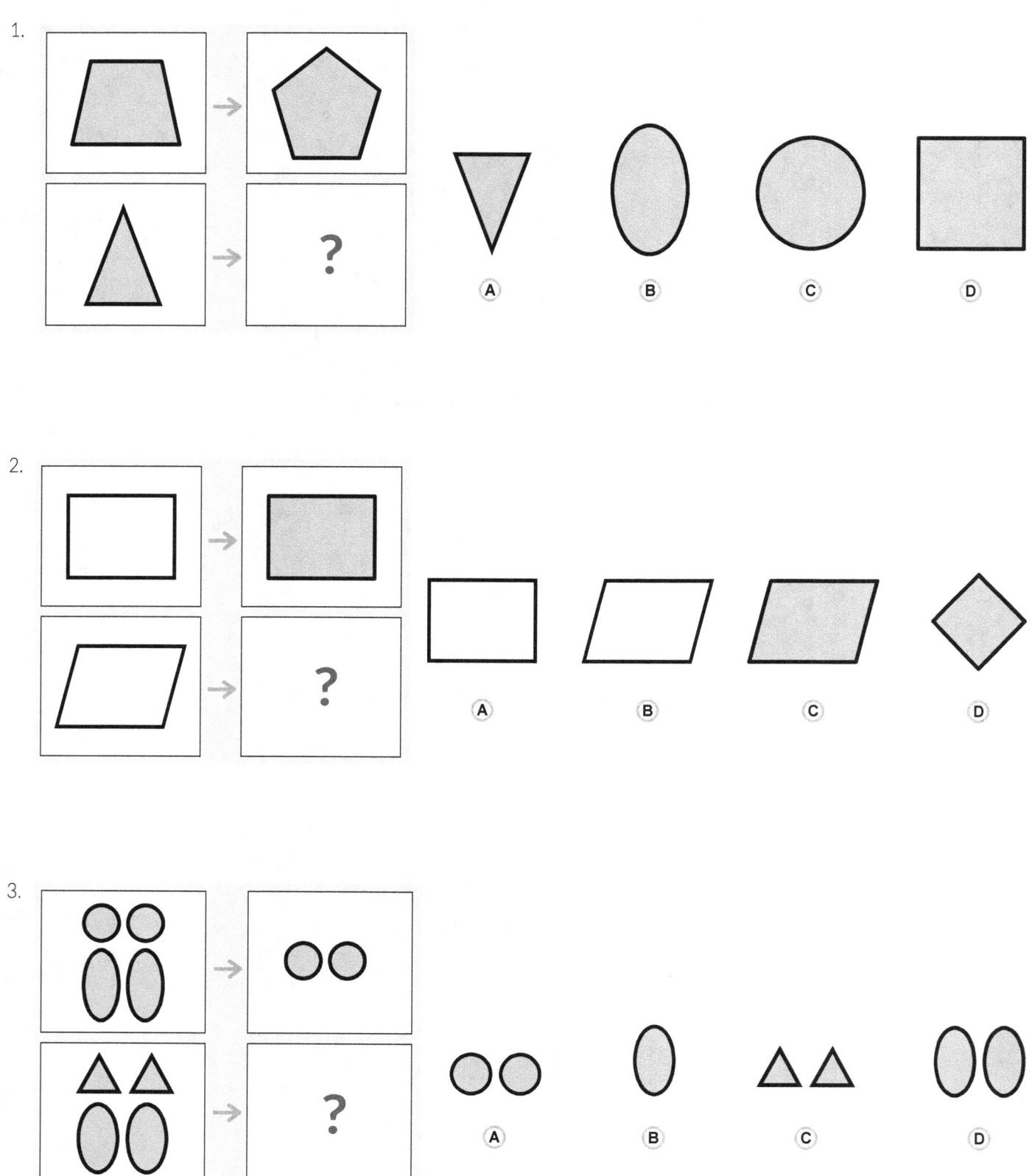

4.

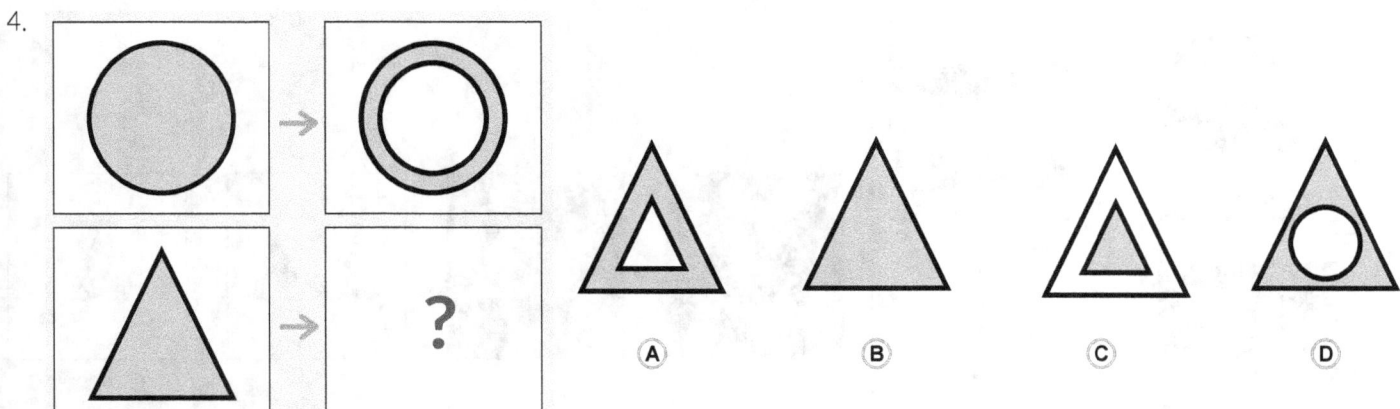

5.

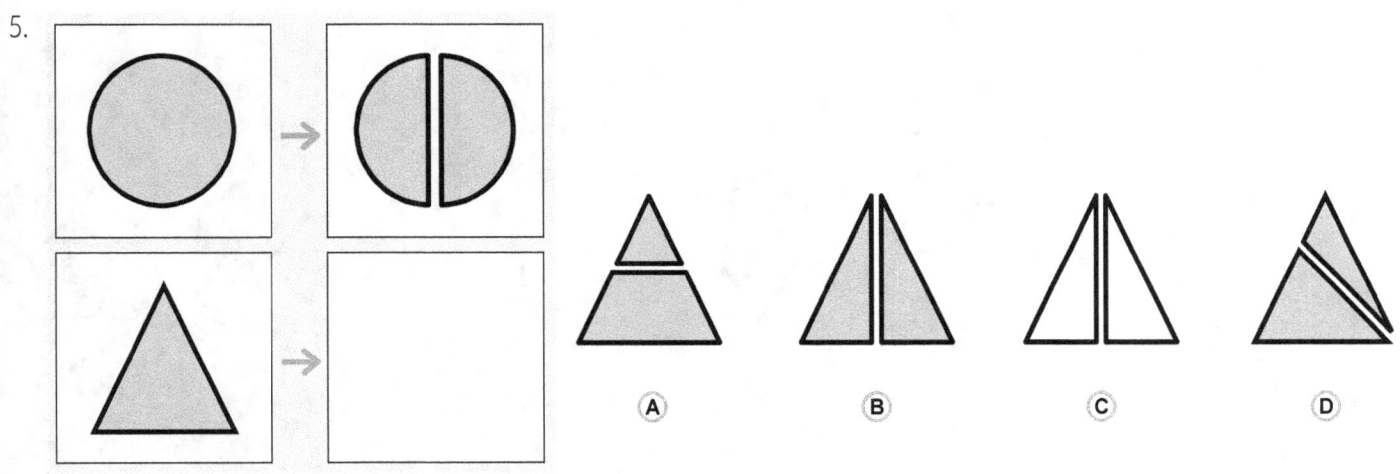

6.

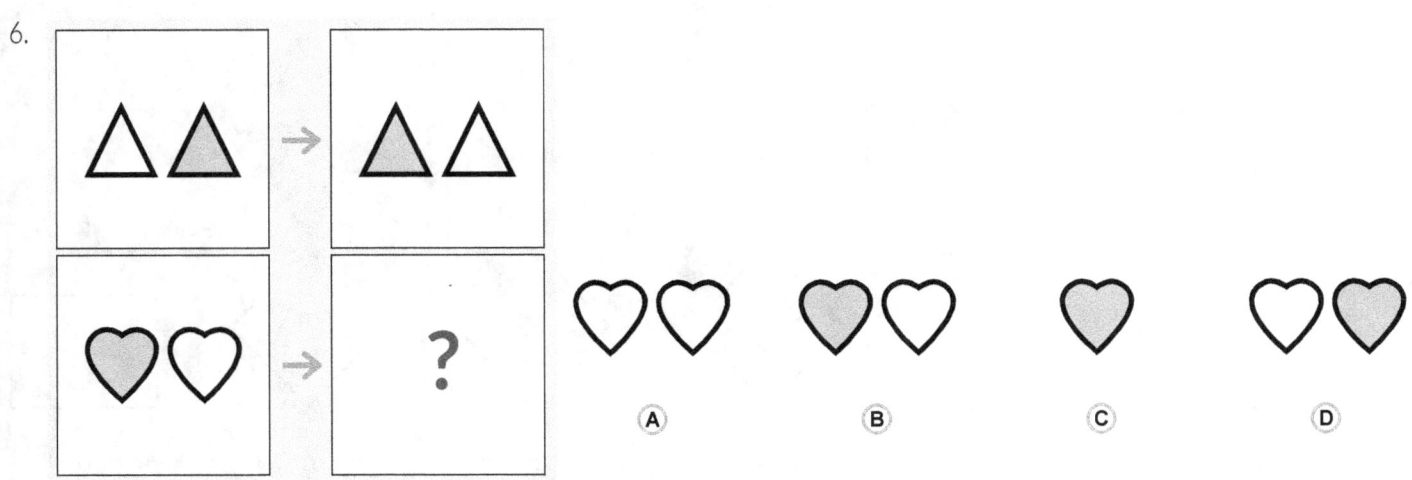

7.

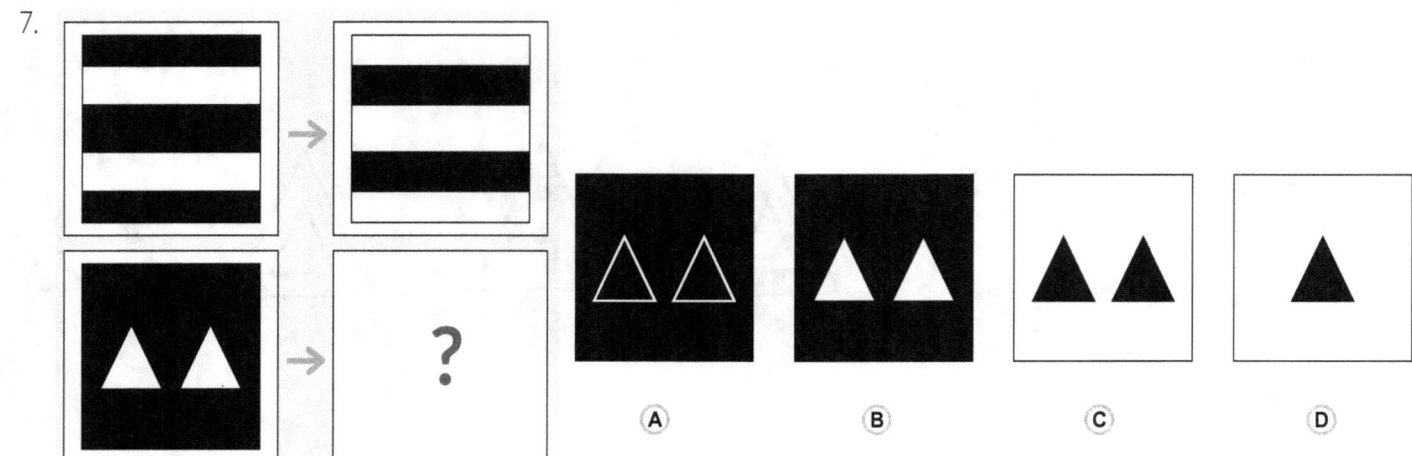

8.

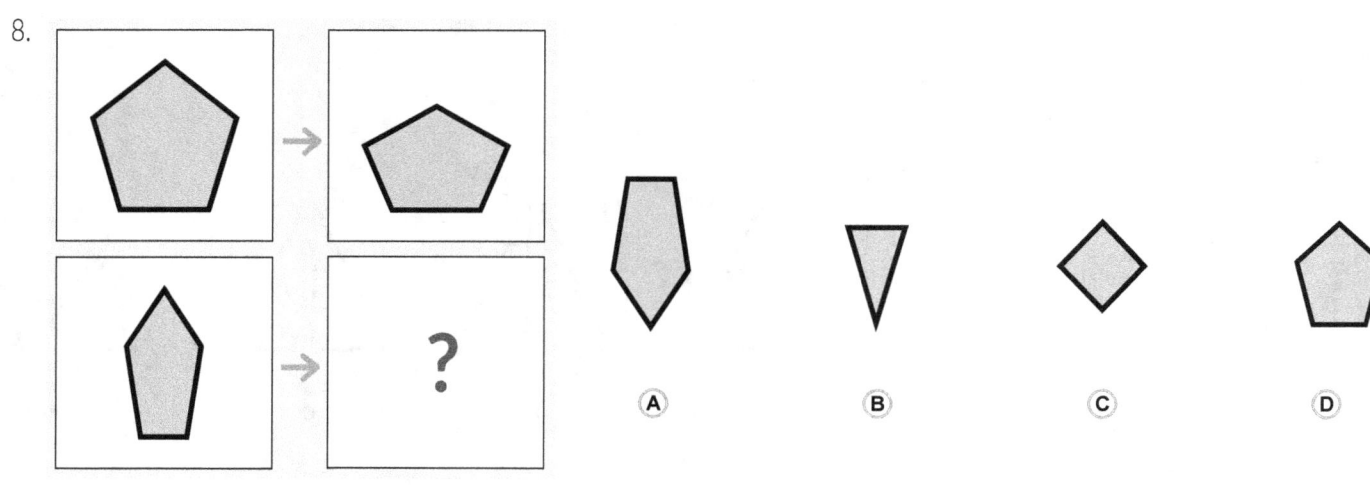

9.

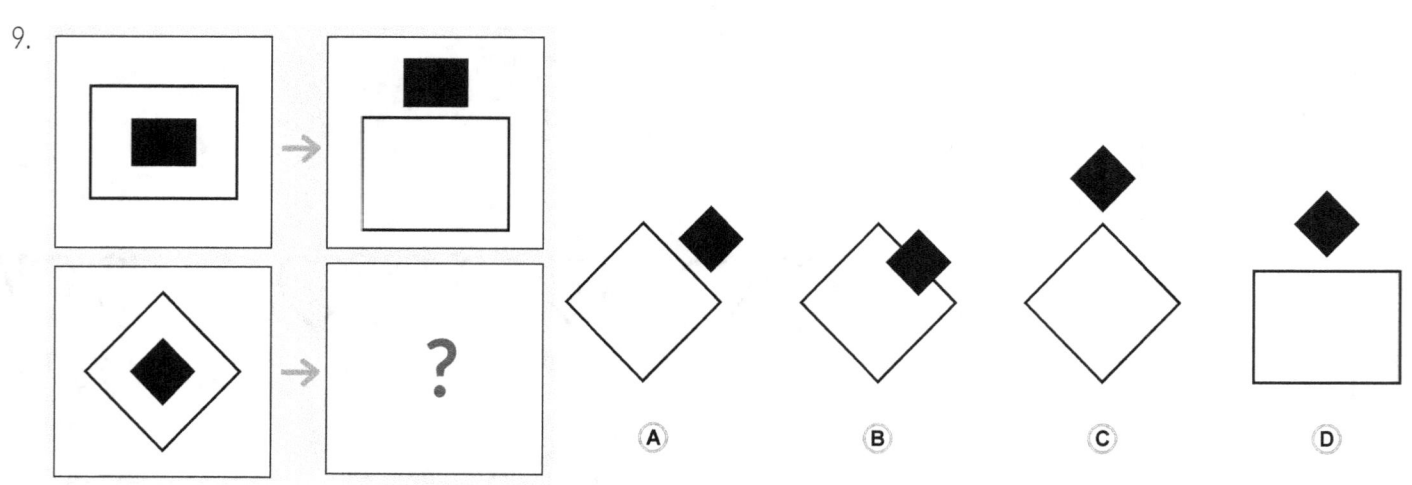

56

10.

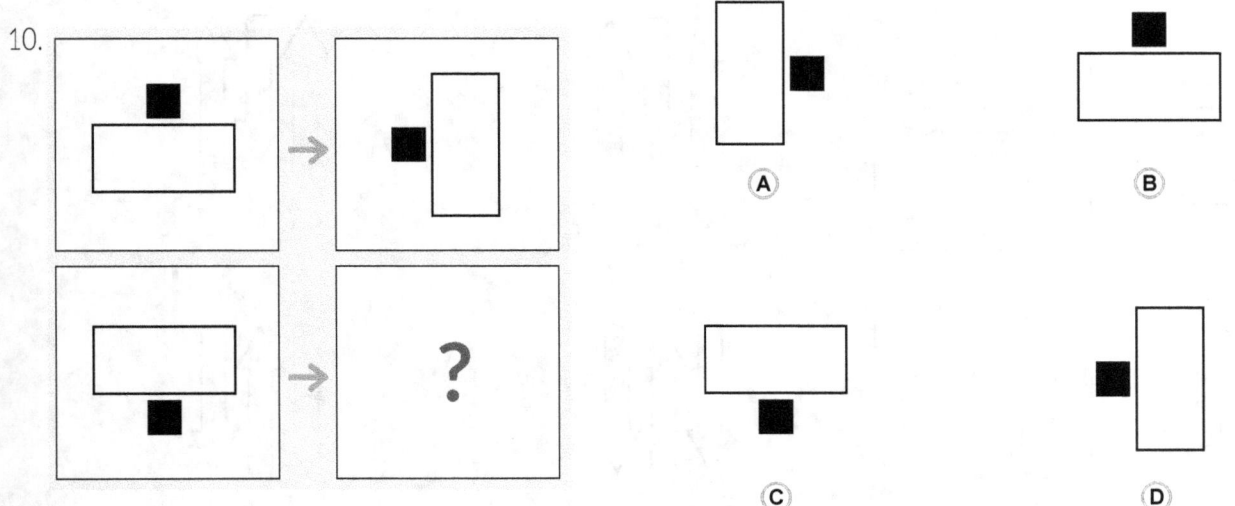

11.

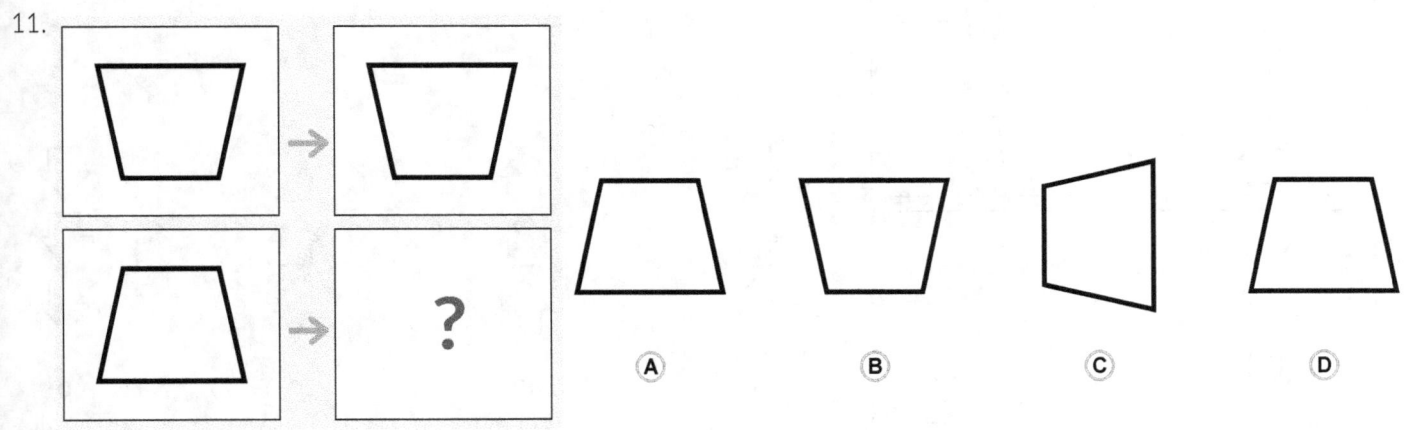

12.

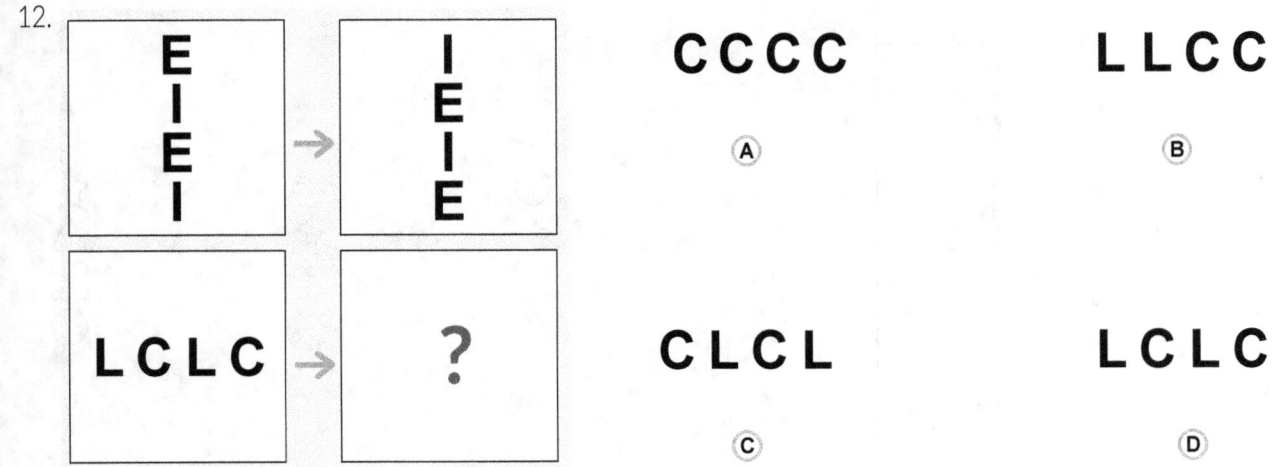

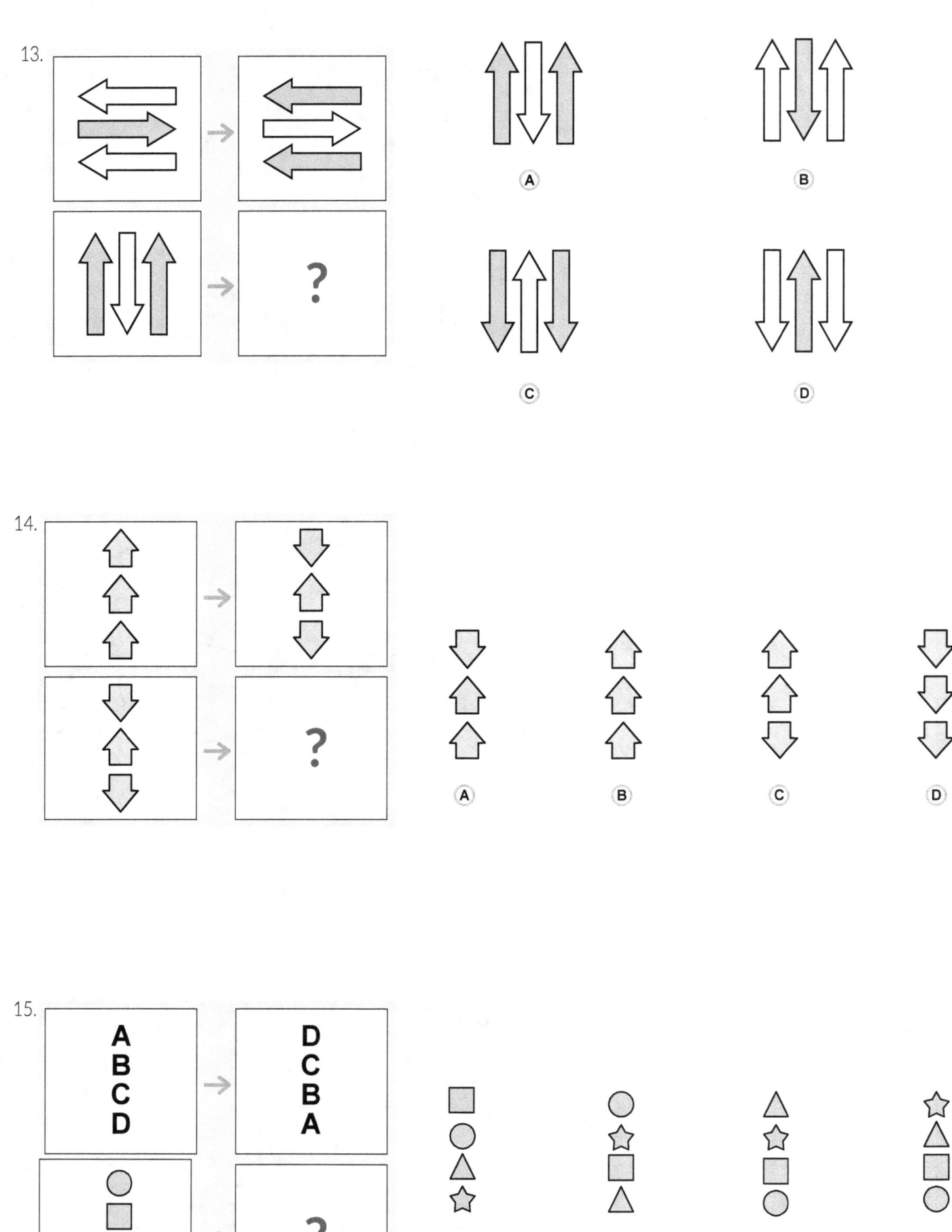

16.

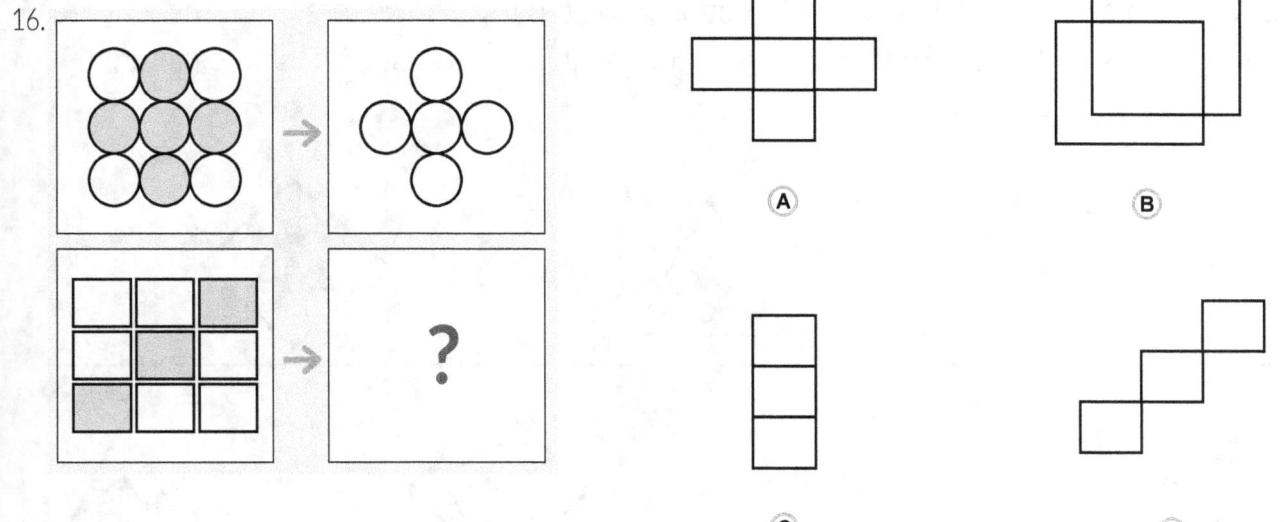

(A) (B) (C) (D)

17.

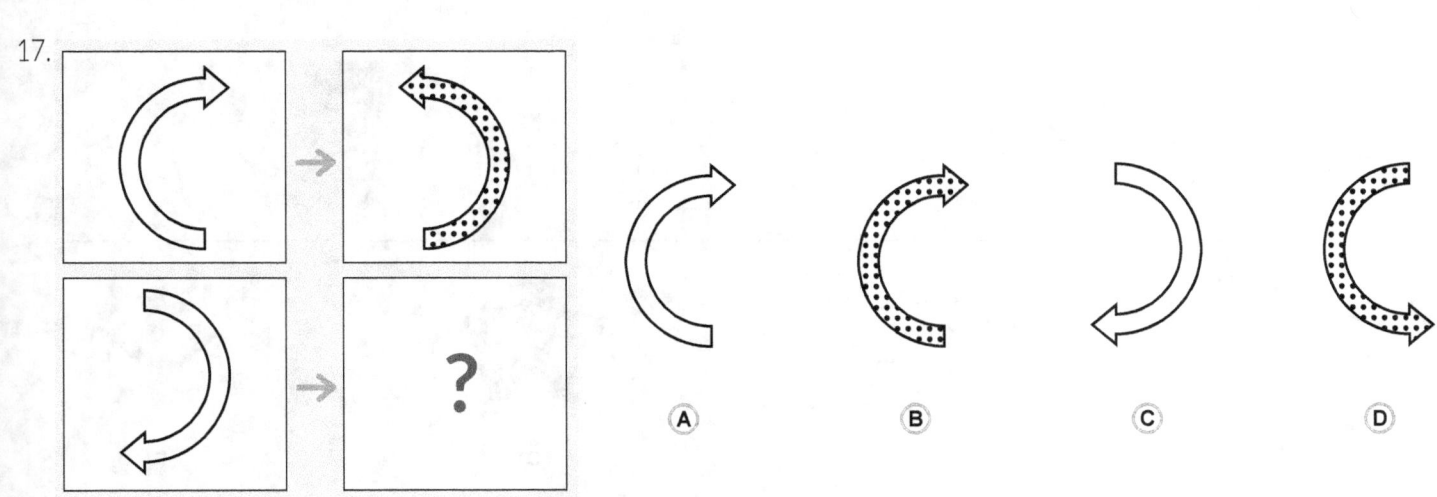

(A) (B) (C) (D)

FIGURE CLASSIFICATION

Directions: The top row shows three pictures that are alike in some way. Look at the bottom row. Which bottom picture goes best with the top pictures?

1.

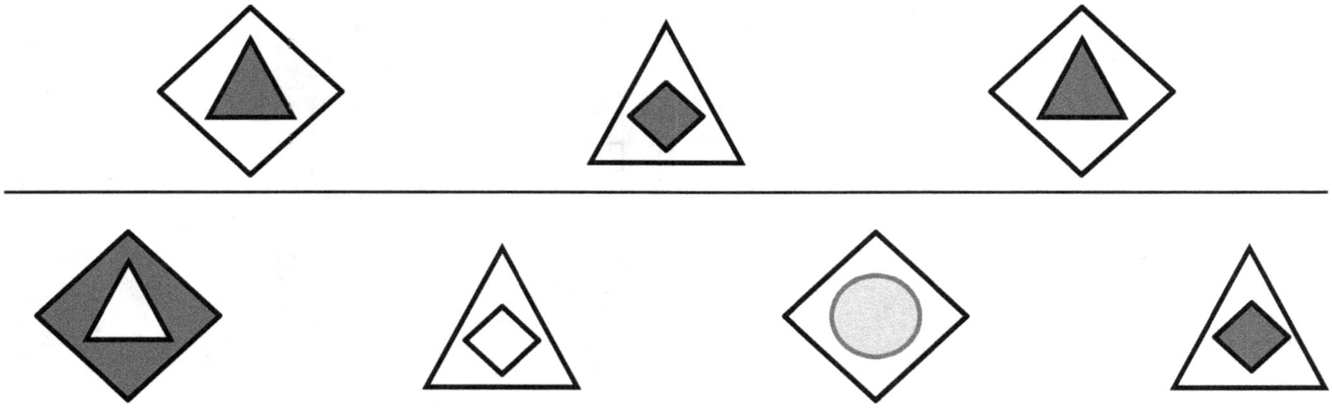

(A)   (B)   (C)   (D)

2.

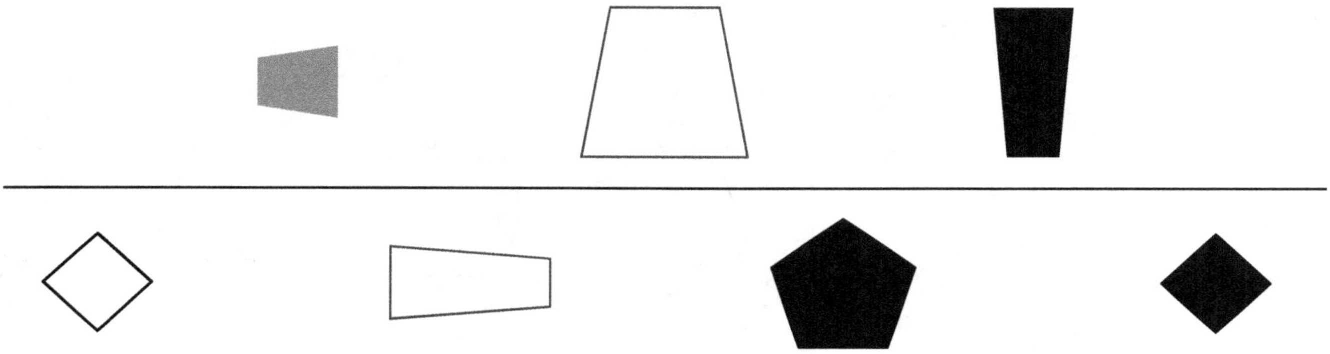

(A)   (B)   (C)   (D)

3.

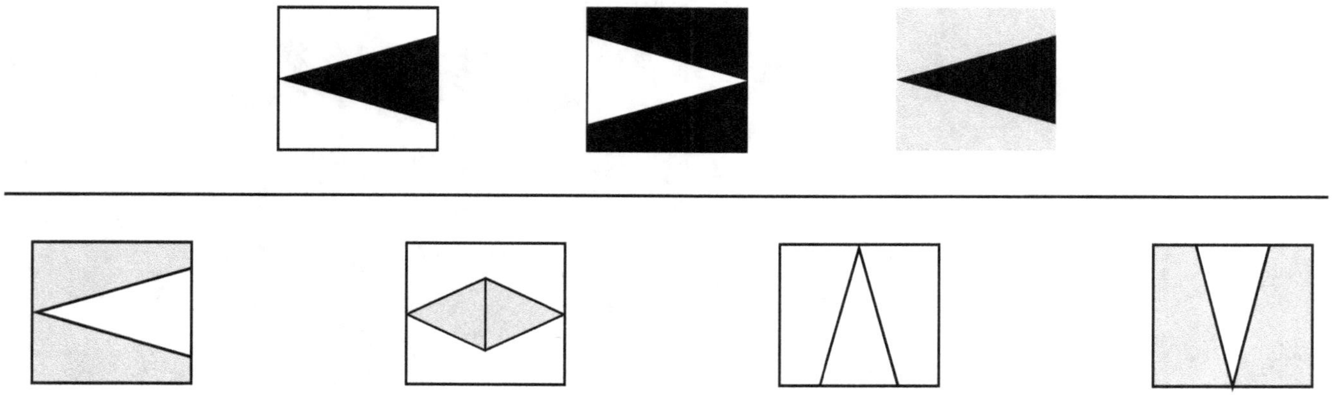

(A)   (B)   (C)   (D)

4.

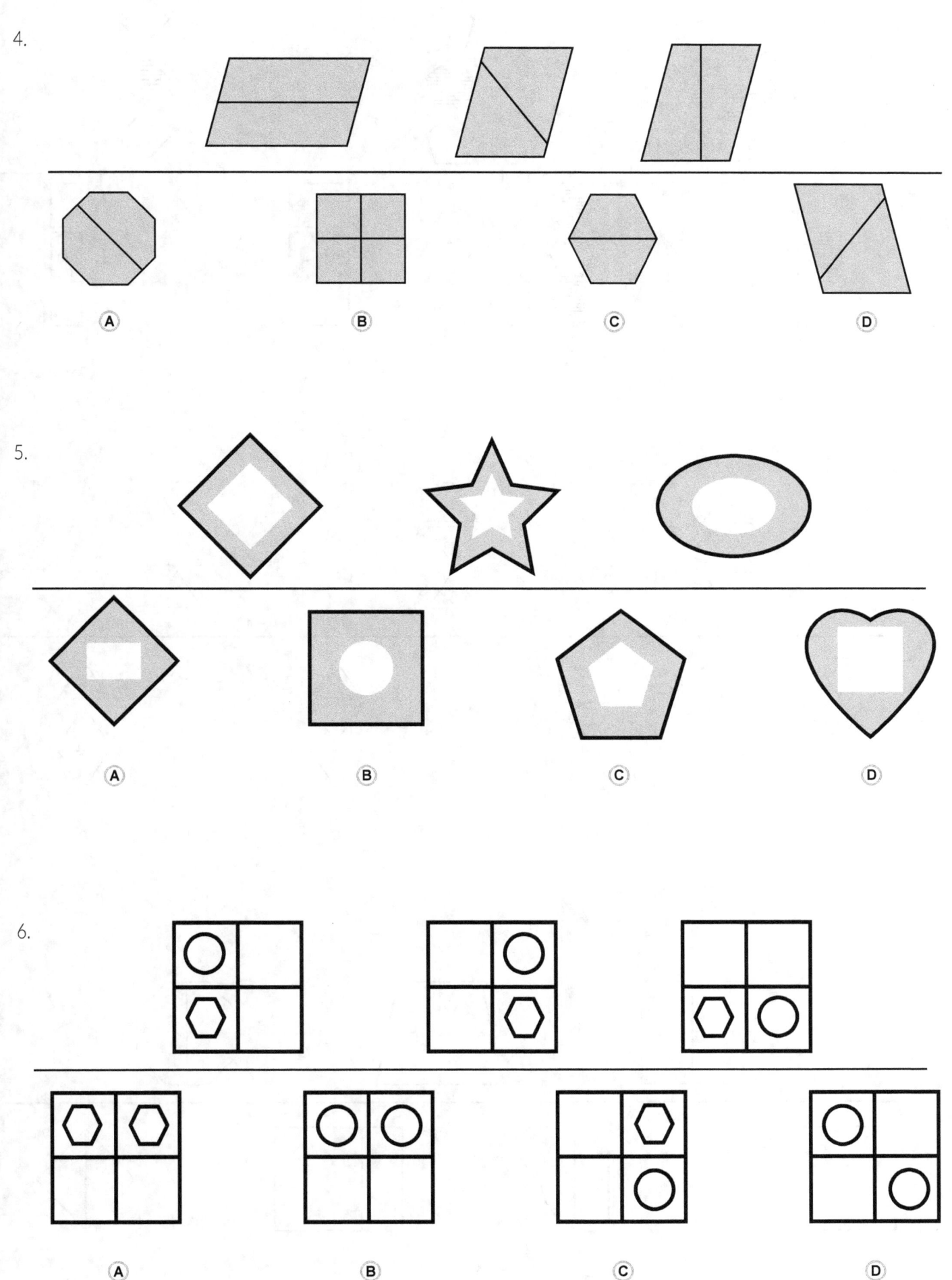

A   B   C   D

5.

A   B   C   D

6.

A   B   C   D

7.

A   B   C   D

8.

A   B   C   D

9.

A   B   C   D

62

10.

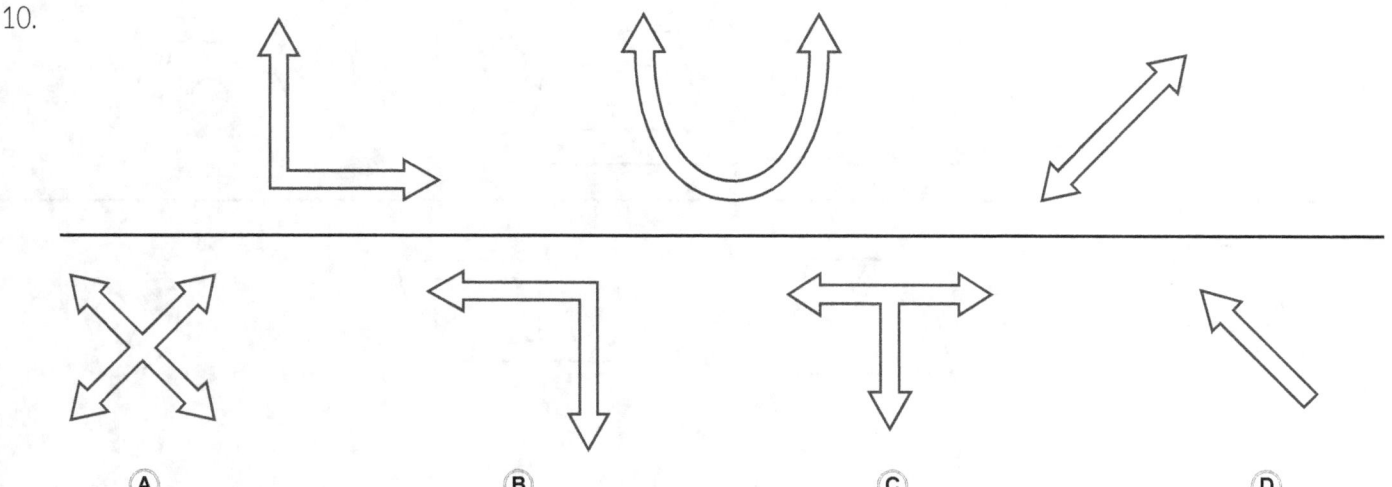

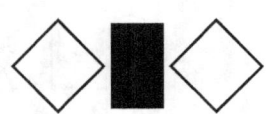      

Ⓐ   Ⓑ   Ⓒ   Ⓓ

11.

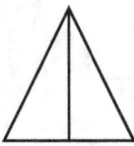   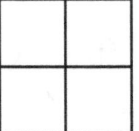

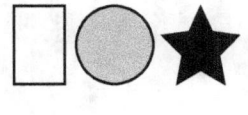   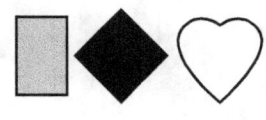      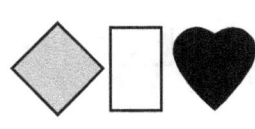

Ⓐ   Ⓑ   Ⓒ   Ⓓ

12.

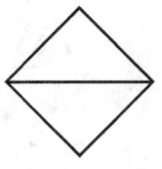   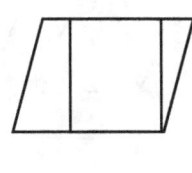   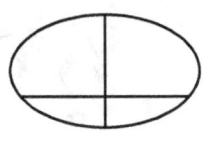   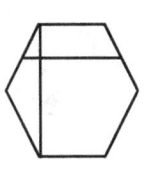

Ⓐ   Ⓑ   Ⓒ   Ⓓ

13.

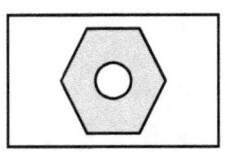 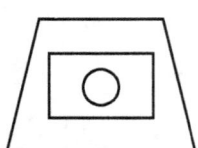 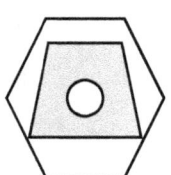

 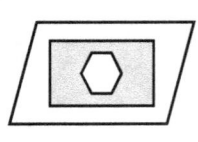 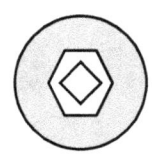

Ⓐ   Ⓑ   Ⓒ   Ⓓ

14.

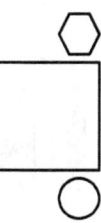 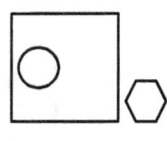

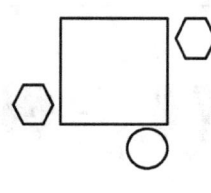 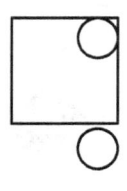 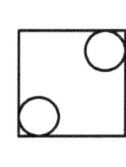

Ⓐ   Ⓑ   Ⓒ   Ⓓ

15.

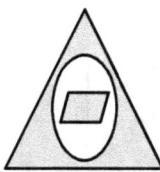 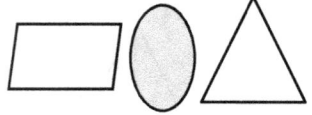

Ⓐ   Ⓑ   Ⓒ   Ⓓ

16.

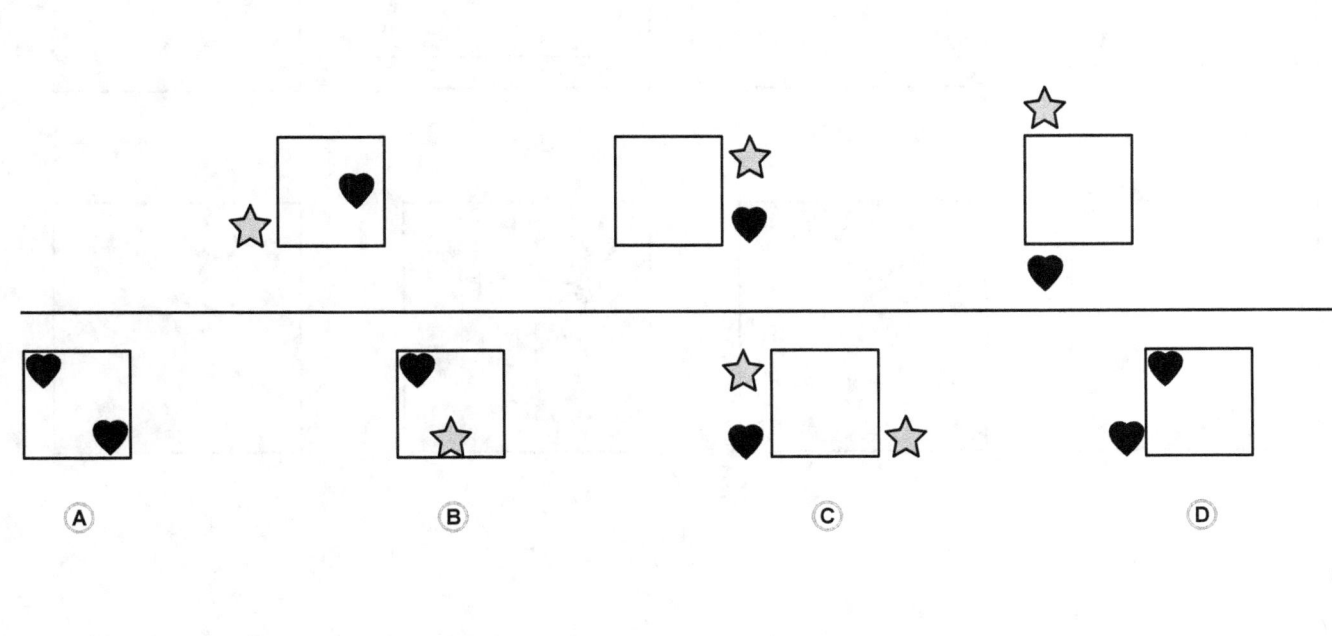

A   B   C   D

17.

A   B   C   D

18.

A   B   C   D

PAPER FOLDING

Which picture in the bottom row shows how the paper would look after it's unfolded?

1.

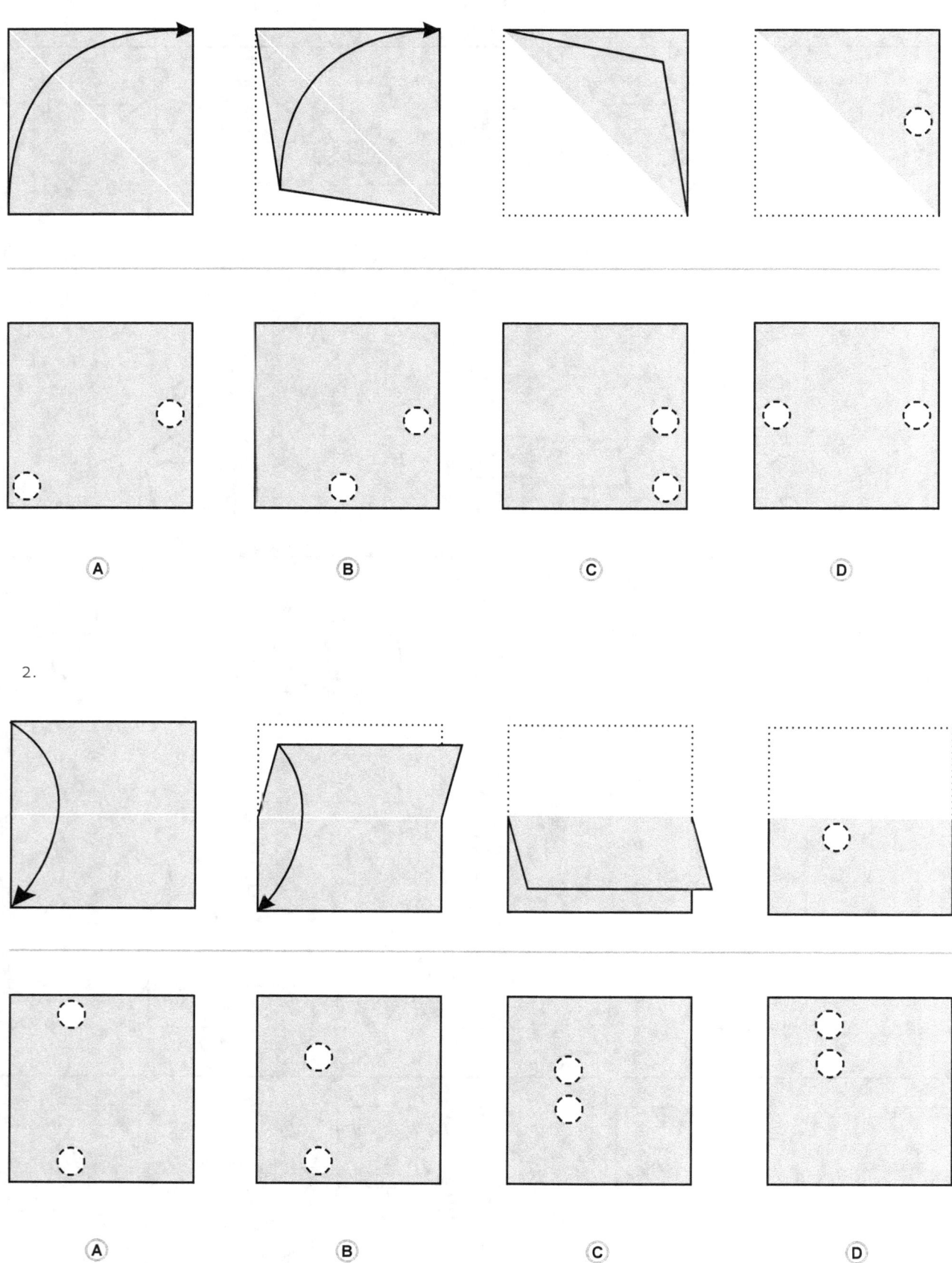

2.

3.

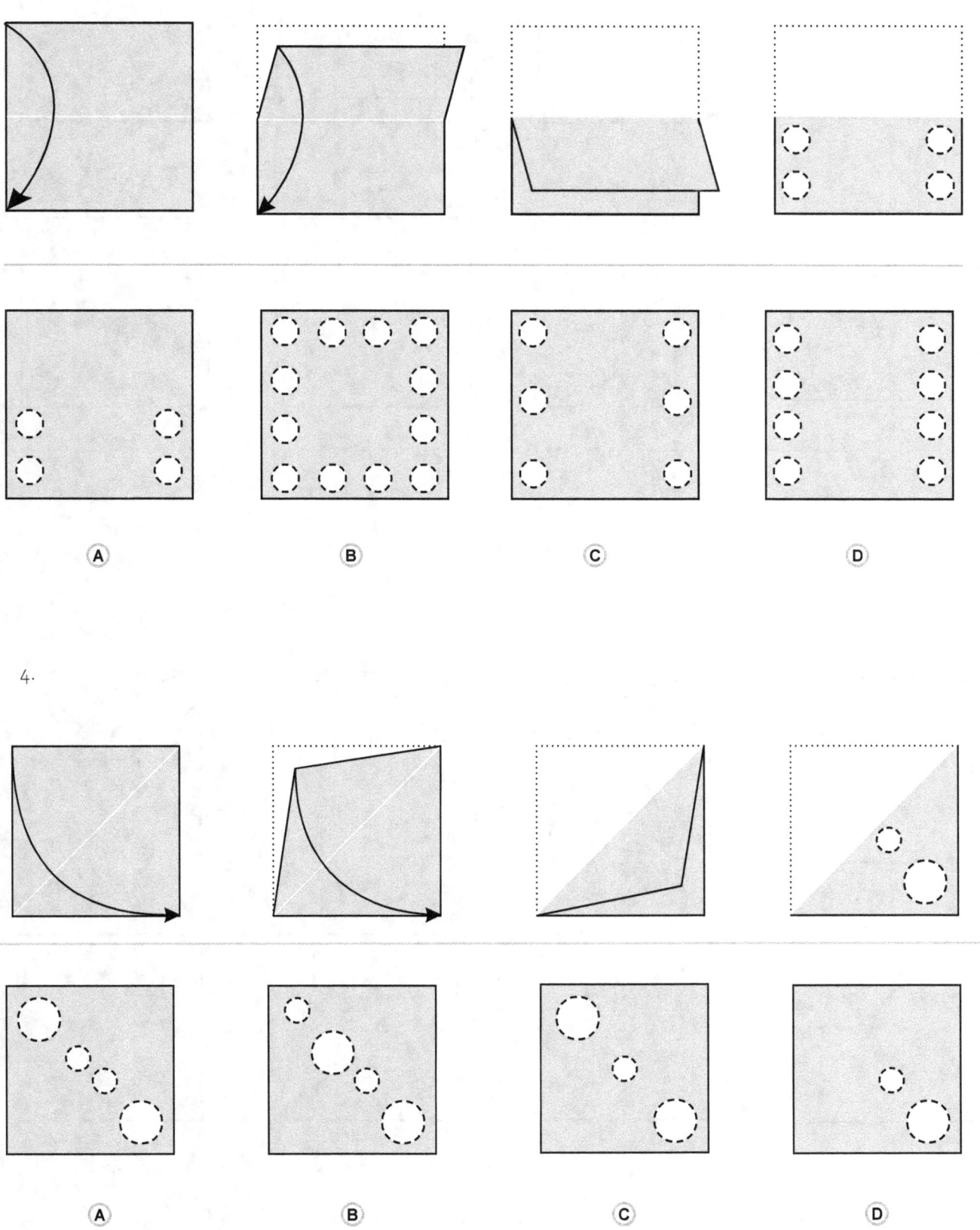

A   B   C   D

4.

A   B   C   D

5.

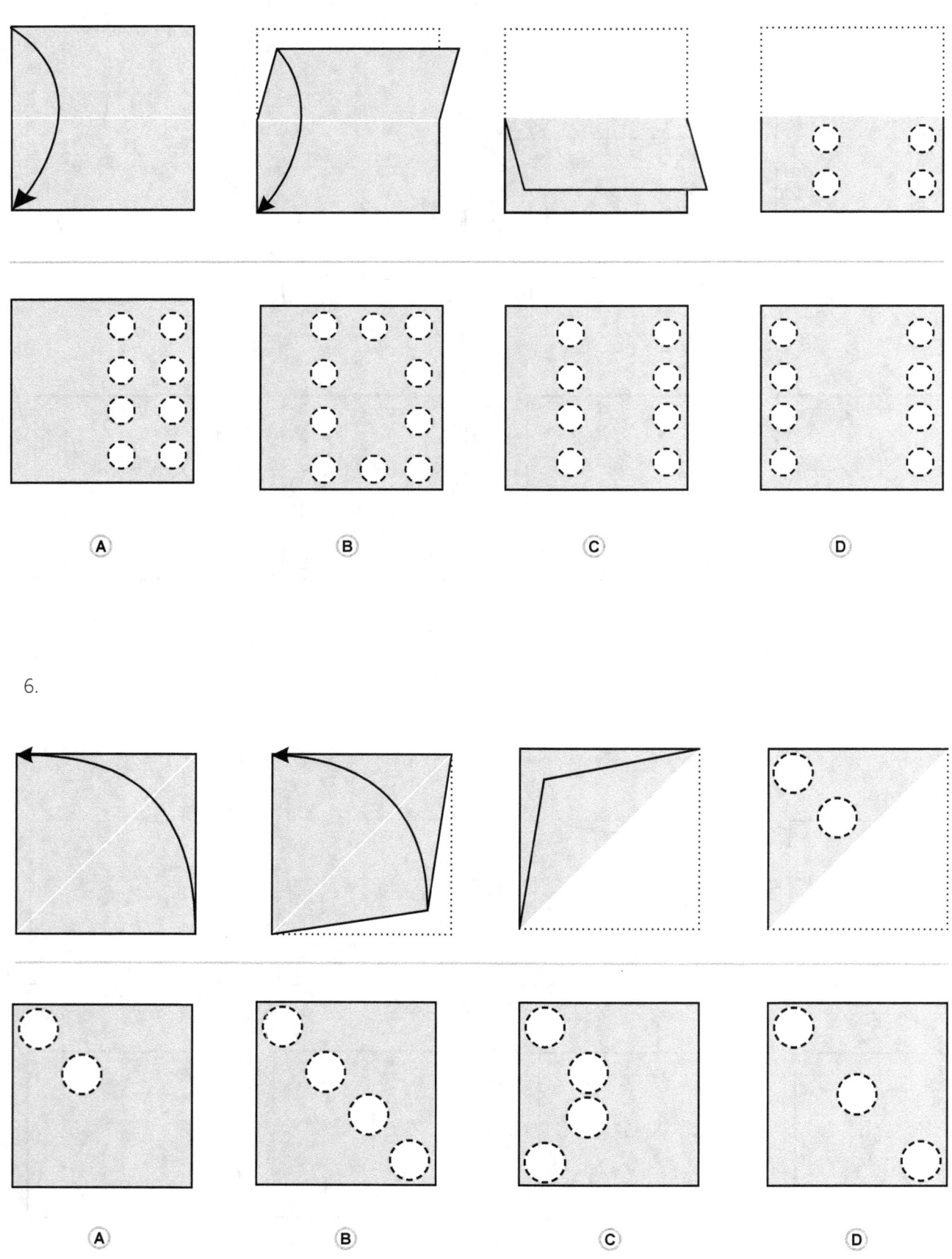

A   B   C   D

6.

A   B   C   D

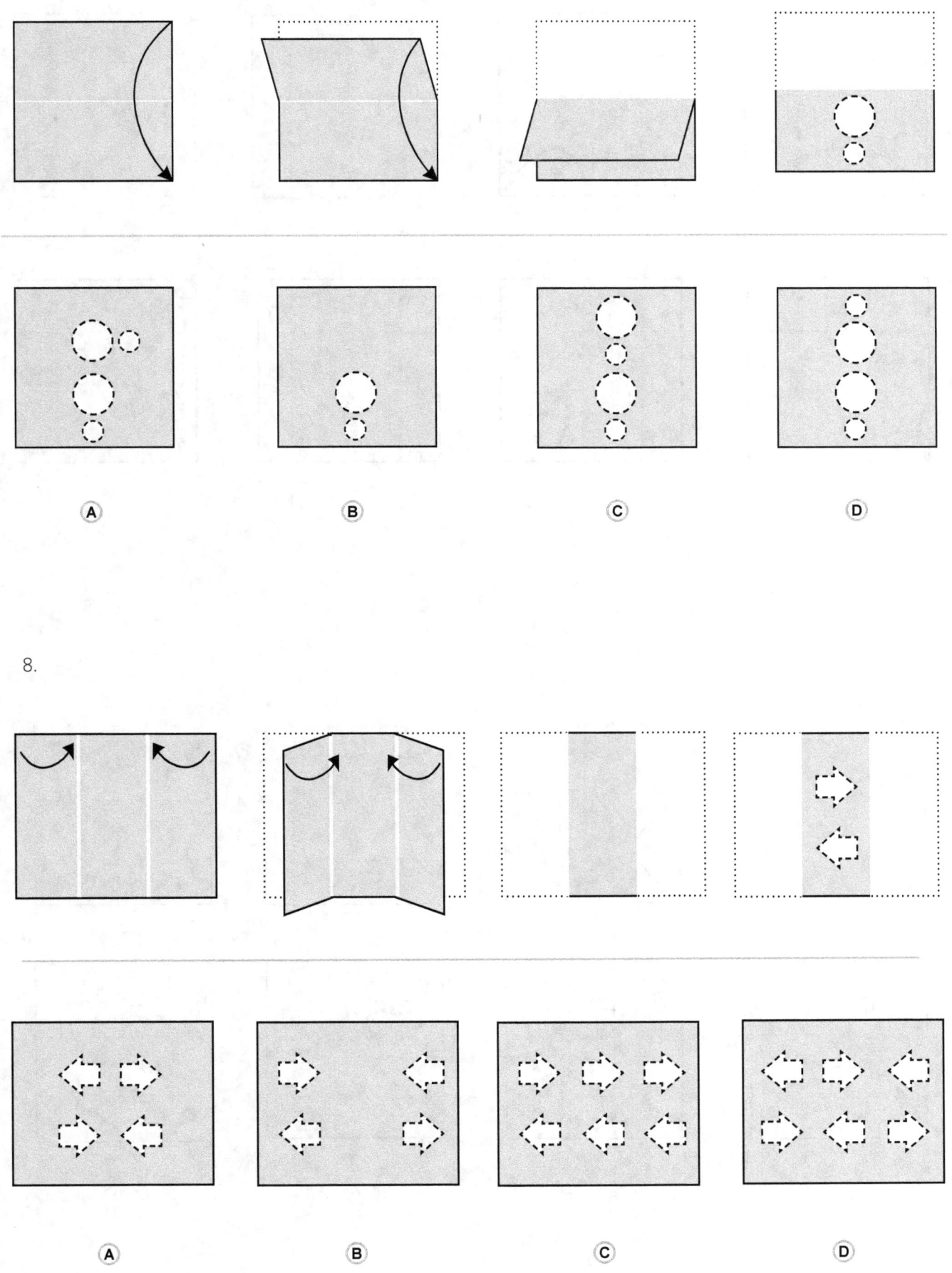

7.

A B C D

8.

A B C D

9.

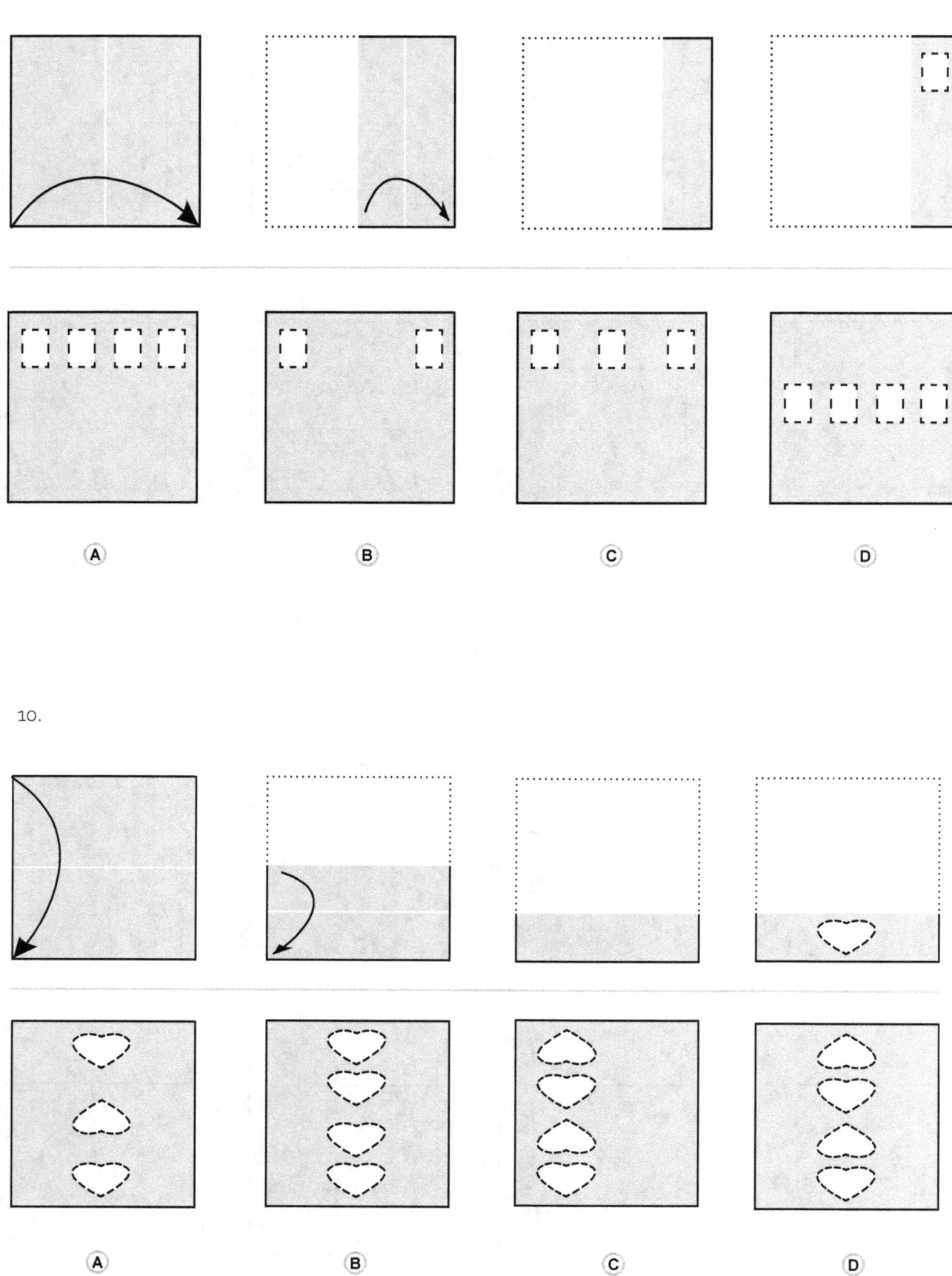

A   B   C   D

10.

A   B   C   D

11.

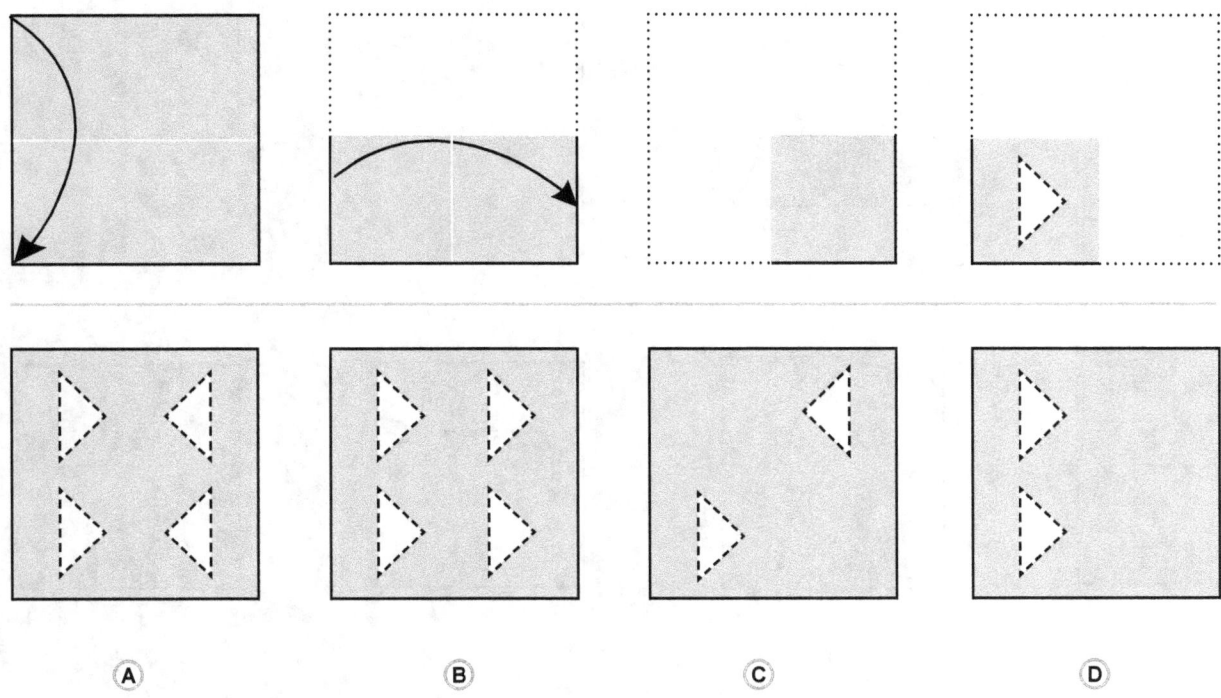

A   B   C   D

12.

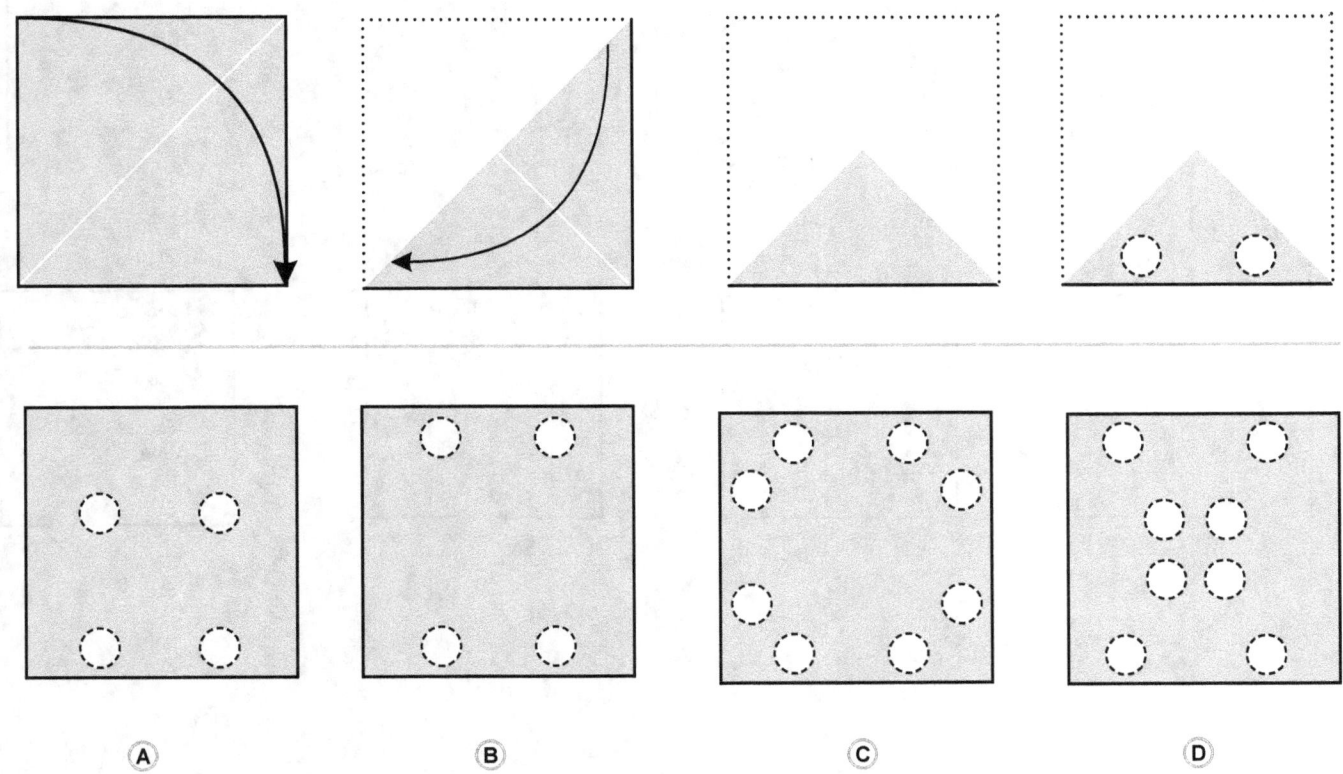

A   B   C   D

13.

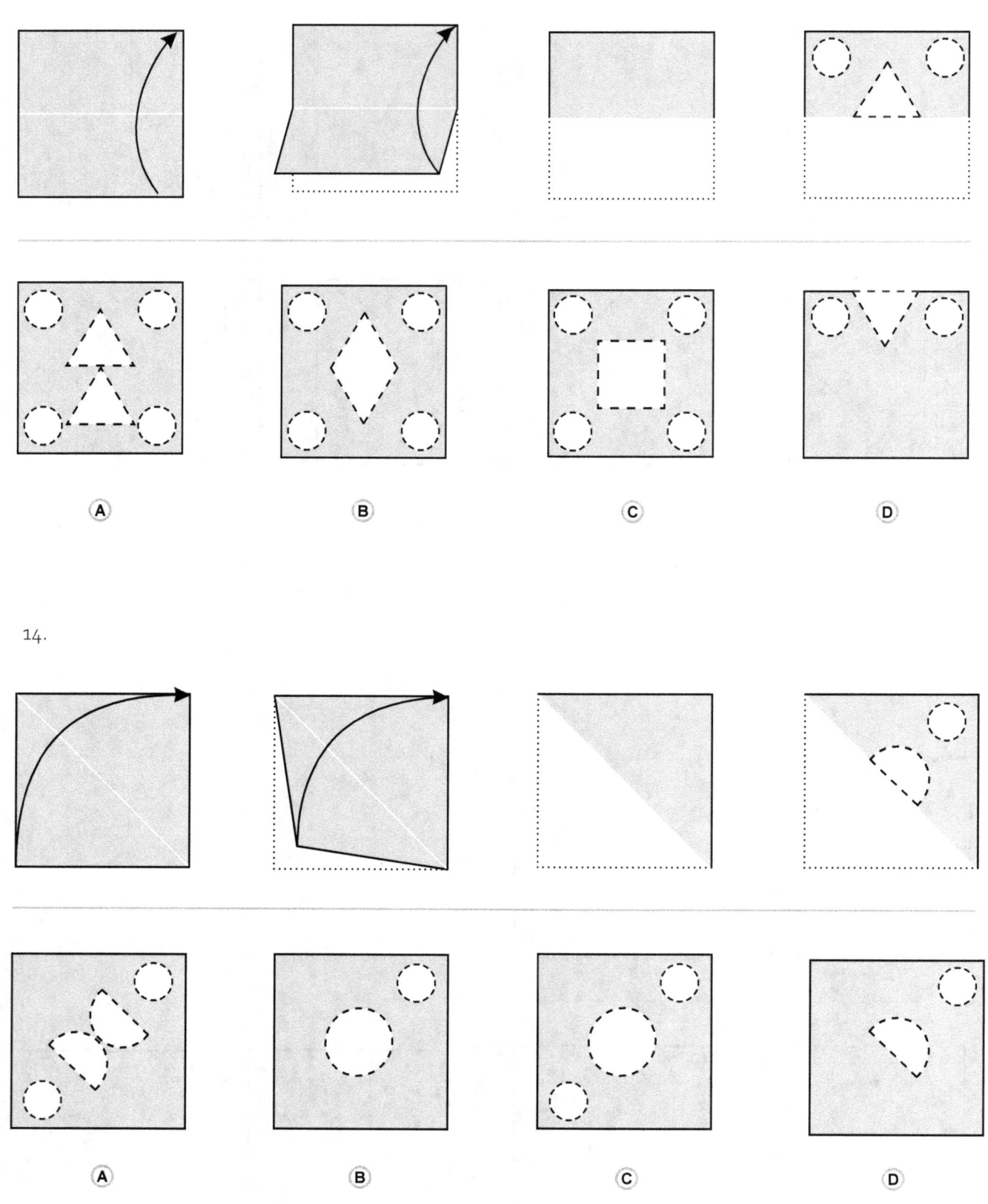

A

B

C

D

14.

A

B

C

D

ANSWER KEYS

ANSWER KEY FOR PRACTICE TEST 1 (WORKBOOK FORMAT)

Figure Analogies, Practice Test 1

-1. C. The bottom half of the shape turns gray.

-2. D. One more shape (the same kind of shape) is added.

-3. D. The colors (black & white) switch.

-4. A. The figure rotates 180 degrees.

-5. C. The figure "flips" to become a mirror image.

-6. D. The shape gets bigger and fills with dots.

-7. B. The shape on the line moves to the opposite side (the right).

-8. A. The smaller, inner shape gets bigger and becomes the outer shape. The larger, outer shape gets smaller and becomes the inner shape.

-9. C. The white shape fills with diagonal lines.

-10. A. The colors gray/black switch. Or, the gray/black shapes themselves switch position.

-11. D. The circles split in half. The left half becomes the color of the original circle. The right half becomes the opposite color.

-12. D. The wand rotates 90 degrees clockwise and turns gray.

-13. C. Stars become hearts. Hearts become stars.

-14. B. The shape in the second box is a 3-D version of the shape in the first box.

-15. B. The shapes switch position (left and right) and color (gray and black).

-16. C. The smaller, inner shape gets bigger and becomes the outer shape. The larger, outer shape gets smaller and becomes the inner shape.

Figure Classification, Practice Test 1

-1. C. The shapes are circles.

-2. B. The shapes are filled with vertical lines.

-3. B. The square has 1 heart and 1 star.

-4. D. The design inside the shapes follow the pattern: vertical lines, white, and vertical lines.

-5. C. The circles have a diagonal line going from the upper left to the lower right.

-6. A. The left heart has vertical lines, and the right heart is white.

-7. B. Three circles in the group are gray, and one is white.

-8. A. There are two of the same shape – one larger gray shape and one smaller black shape.

-9. A. The shapes have 4 sides and are divided in half.

-10. D. The shapes have diagonal lines going from upper left to lower right.

-11. C. The arrows either point left or right.

-12. D. There are two of the same shape – one larger gray shape and one smaller white shape.

-13. A. The shapes are divided in half.

-14. B. There are 2 up arrows and 1 down arrow.

-15. B. Half of the circle is black and half is white.

-16. D. The shapes have a triangle as the smallest center shape.

Paper Folding, Practice Test 1

-1. B	-2. C	-3. D	-4. A	-5. A	-6. B
-7. D	-8. A	-9. D	-10. B	-11. A	-12. C
-13. D	-14. A	-15. B	-16. D	-17. C	

ANSWER KEY FOR PRACTICE TEST 2

Figure Analogies, Practice Test 2

-1. C. A smaller, white version of the original gray shape appears in the middle of the original shape.

-2. A. The shape gets bigger and turns black.

-3. B. The shape divides in half horizontally, and the top half fills with wavy lines.

-4. A. The arrow rotates 90 degrees clockwise.

-5. D. The heart rotates 180 degrees.

-6. C. The diagonal lines in the shape change from going from the upper left to the lower right. In the second box, the diagonal lines go from the lower left to the upper right. Or, the shape "flips" and becomes a mirror image of the original shape.

-7. D. The smaller shape moves to the right side of the line.

-8. A. The shape is divided in half. The lower half changes from gray to filled with dots.

-9. A. The position of the letters switch (O and U; T and E).

-10. D. Circles change to X's, and X's change to circles.

-11. C. The shape in the second box is a 3-D version of the shape in the first box.

-12. B. The shapes switch positions.

-13. C. The shapes switch position (left and right) and color (gray and white).

-14. C. The small, black center shape gets larger.

-15. A. The colors (white and gray) switch.

Figure Classification, Practice Test 2

-1. B. There are 3 of the same kind of shape. The inner design is: gray, wavy lines, gray.

-2. C. In the divided square, the two shapes on the left and right are the same kind of shape.

-3. A. The shape group is aligned vertically. There are two smaller versions on the top and bottom of the larger middle shape.

-4. B. The shapes have horizontal lines inside.

-5. D. The rectangles are divided in half. One half is gray, and the other is filled with dots.

-6. B. There are 2 (and only 2) shapes filled with dots – 1 oval and 1 square.

-7. C. Half of the diamond is filled with dots.

-8. C. There are 2 triangles pointing up and 1 triangle pointing down.

-9. B. There are 4 shapes in the group.

-10. A. There are 3 black squares. Two black squares are next to each other and the other one touches one corner of the group of 2.

-11. B. The shapes have 6 sides.

-12. A. Inside the circles are 4 lines.

-13. C. The shape group has 2 shapes that are the same and one that's different.

-14. B. In the middle of the light gray square is one star.

-15. D. As the arrow rotates, the black octagon stays in the same position on the arrow (by the dotted line).

Paper Folding, Practice Test 2

| -1. A | -2. D | -3. A | -4. C | -5. B | -6. C | -7. D |
| -8. B | -9. A | -10. B | -11. C | -12. A | -13. D | -14. B |

ANSWER KEY FOR PRACTICE TEST 3

Figure Analogies, Practice Test 3

-1. D. A shape with one more side appears in the second box. On top, there is a trapezoid (4 sides), followed by a pentagon (5 sides). On bottom, there is a triangle (3 sides), followed by a square (4 sides).

-2. C. The shape becomes gray.

-3. C. The bottom ovals disappear.

-4. A. A slightly smaller white version of the original shape appears in the center of the original shape.

-5. B. The shape is cut in half vertically.

-6. D. The shapes switch colors. Or, the shapes flip to become a mirror image of the original.

-7. C. The colors switch. (Black becomes white, and white becomes black).

-8. D. The shape in the second box is a shorter, flatter version of the original shape.

-9. C. The middle black shape moves above the larger white shape.

-10. A. The shape group rotates 90 degrees counterclockwise.

-11. A. The same shape is in the second box.

-12. C. The letters switch positions.

-13. B. The colors (gray and white) switch.

-14. B. The top and bottom arrows rotate 180 degrees. Also, note that the arrow groups in the opposite boxes (top right & bottom left -and- top left & bottom right) are the same.

-15. D. The letters & shapes reverse order.

-16. D. The shapes that remain are those that are gray in the first box.

-17. D. The arrow "flips" (becomes a mirror image) and fills with dots.

-1. D. The shape group has either: 1 large white diamond & 1 small darker triangle or 1 large white triangle & 1 small darker diamond.

-2. B. The shapes are the same kind of shape (trapezoids).

-3. A. There is only one triangle inside the squares that either points left or right.

-4. D. The 4-sided shapes have 1 line inside.

-5. C. There are two of the same shape – one larger gray shape and one smaller white shape.

-6. C. The square has 1 circle and 1 hexagon.

-7. A. There are 3 of the same kind of shape in this order: white, horizontal lines, white.

-8. D. There are 2 triangles pointing up and 1 triangle pointing down.

-9. D. The shapes are divided in half.

-10. B. The arrows have 2 arrow points.

-11. C. There are 2 shapes of the same type & color on the left and right.

There is 1 shape of another type & color in the middle.

-12. A. The shapes are divided into equal parts (either half or quarters).

-13. B. There is a small white circle in the middle of the shape group.

-14. A. Each group has: 1 large square, 1 (and only 1) small hexagon, and 1 (and only 1) small circle.

-15. D. The shape group is made up of a triangle, an oval, and a parallelogram.

-16. D. As the shape group rotates, the white circle stays at the same spot on the arrow point.

(Note that choice B and C are not correct. You can find the same gray arrows in the top row, but the white circle is not at the same spot. Choice A has the circle in the wrong spot as well.)

continues on the next page

-17. A. There are 3 (and only 3) shapes in the group.

-18. B. The shape group is made up of a white square, 1 (and only 1) gray star, and 1 (and only 1) black heart.

Paper Folding, Practice Test 3

| -1. B | -2. C | -3. D | -4. A | -5. C | -6. B | -7. D |
| -8. D | -9. A | -10. D | -11. A | -12. C | -13. B | -14. C |

Need more practice?

- Help your child **ace the test**!

- Check out **Savant Test Prep**™ books on Amazon®.